What Others Are Saying About Sharing Nature

"The first edition of this book sparked a worldwide revolution in nature education and became a classic." —**National Association for Interpretation**

"Joseph Cornell was one of the first to anticipate the need for opening the doors for children and families to maintain and refresh their connection with the natural world. His long-standing work and vision have nourished the roots of the emerging worldwide movement to reconnect children and nature."—**Cheryl Charles, PhD,** Co-Founder, President, and CEO Emerita, Children & Nature Network

"I found *Sharing Nature with Children* a most original and imaginative concept in a field which is vital for the welfare of the planet."
—**Sir Peter Scott,** conservationist, a founder of World Wide Fund for Nature

"Joseph Cornell is one of the most highly regarded nature educators in the world today." —*Backpacker* **magazine**

"By using the activities . . . the child actually experiences what it is like to be part of the natural world." —**National Audubon Society**

"Absolutely the best awareness of nature book I've ever seen."
—*Whole Earth Review*

"How pleasant it is to find a guidebook, written with such sensitivity, that helps parents or teachers share their love of nature with a child."
—**The Nature Conservancy**

"I wish there had been such a superb book on nature education when I was at school." —**Tom Burke,** Friends of the Earth

"I like this book immensely. It is just the sort of book to fire young imaginations and turn dull ditchwater of conventional education into exciting rivers." —**Phil Drabble,** English author and TV host

"The games nurture children's tendency to regard the world with wonder, and they remind us, as adults, of ways to experience the joy and expansion of being one and at home with our Earth."

—**Alexandra Dowd,** *One Earth* magazine

"In the late 1970s, Cornell's book introduced 'nature games' in which nature is the teacher—games that inform, inspire, and are just plain fun. Almost two decades later . . . *Sharing Nature* has become not just a book but a worldwide approach to nature education."

—**Planet Patriot Books**

Other Books by Joseph Bharat Cornell

"*Listening to Nature* is a splendid masterpiece that captures the 'Oneness' we are all seeking to achieve with Nature."

—**Tom Brown, Jr.,** author of *The Tracker*

"Gives people a dynamic experience of their unity with the natural world." —**Alaska Natural History Association**

"A work of art and of the heart!"

—**Candace Sibcy,** naturalist and nature photographer

"As a teacher, naturalist, and storyteller, I have used Joseph Cornell's Sharing Nature books as the core of much of my work. Now, with *The Sky and Earth Touched Me,* Joseph shows how to connect with nature on an even deeper level. This book is an instructional manual for all who wish to live in harmony with Planet Earth." —**Frank Helling,** U.S. National Park naturalist, John Muir storyteller, and educator

"The same spirit of playful mindfulness that Joseph Cornell has used to connection millions of children with the outdoors he now offers to us all. This book is a gift!" —**Bill Mckibben,** founder 350.org, environmentalist

"Rather than taking strolls in the woods, we become the woods. Cornell inspires our transformation by greatly helping us shed what separates us from nature." —**Tamarack Song,** author, *Entering the Mind of the Tracker*

"*The Sky and the Earth Touched Me* invites you to personally experience the same joy of nature we are trying to instill in our youth. His new book speaks directly to the individual adult reader. With beautiful, soul-provoking quotations and photographs, interwoven with heartfelt, profound exercises, readers are prompted to experience nature's beauty, tranquility, and love.

"Whether you are a novice or an experienced naturalist, let this book be your companion while exploring nature. It will increasingly deepen your appreciation, relationship, and spirituality with the natural world."
          —**Roy Simpson,** Education Specialist, Bureau of Land Management

"This man is connected to the heart of our planet, and the Earth's wisdom shines through him." —**New Texas Magazine**

"*The Sky and Earth Touched Me* offers a chance to experience nature's wonders deep within ourselves. Joseph Cornell's outdoor activities are a delight, showing both children and adults how to see and experience nature in ways they might not have thought possible. Imagine the lines of distinction between you and a tree or animal becoming blurred or disappearing altogether, as you realize you have become that tree or animal in a very real sense. Read the book and be inspired; do the activities and be transformed!"
          —**Kathryn Gann,** Director, Theosophical Society of America

"Joseph Cornell has a gift for sensitizing others to their natural world— and to their inner world."
          —**Douglas Wood,** author of *Grandad's Prayers of the Earth*

"I have always had a sincere love for nature. Your workshop brought that love to a level I never dreamed possible. I wish I could have experienced a Sharing Nature Workshop earlier in my career."
          —**Joseph T. Emerick,** Environmental Education Coordinator,
                    Cambria Co. Conservation District, Pennsylvania

"Reverence and respect for the nature life forces permeates Joseph Cornell's writings. He shares . . . ways to experience the joy and expansion of being one and at home with our Earth." —*One Earth* **magazine**

"Joseph Cornell has had a towering, phenomenal influence on the development of environmental education in Central Europe."
—**F. W. Georg,** founding director of the
Nature Conservancy Academy, Hessen, Germany

SHARING NATURE®

Nature Awareness Activities
for All Ages

JOSEPH CORNELL

Crystal Clarity Publishers
Nevada City, California

Printed in China

1 3 5 7 9 10 8 6 4 2

ISBN-13: 978-1-56589-287-3
ePub ISBN: 978-1-56589-554-6

Cover design, interior design and layout by Tejindra Scott Tully

---

Library of Congress Cataloging-in-Publication Data

Cornell, Joseph Bharat.
  Sharing nature : nature awareness activities for all ages / Joseph
Bharat Cornell. -- 1st ed.
      pages cm.
  Includes index.
  ISBN 978-1-56589-287-3 (quality paperback)
    ISBN 978-1-56589-554-6 (epub)
1. Nature study--Activity programs. 2. Natural history--Study and
teaching (Early childhood) I. Title.

  QH54.5.C67 2014
  507.8--dc23

                                    2014007590

 www.crystalclarity.com / 800.424.1055 — 530.478.7600

CONTENTS

Foreword

Nearby or far away, experiences in the natural world bring us *alive*. Recall, if you will, those moments when you were outdoors, moving, doing, learning, fully using your senses, feeling truly joyful. Those may have been rare events—though I hope that's not the case—but if you were lucky enough to experience such moments, they remain indelible in memory. They hold life within them. When you recall those moments, you feel, once again, that deep sense of wonder and possibility.

What if there were a method to reinstate this feeling of authenticity in *others*? That was the question educator Joseph Cornell asked himself in 1971.

It's no easy task to develop a nature-based teaching method capable of awakening a deep sense of awe and possibility in a swarm of active children, but Cornell did just that. He created a powerful brand of nature-based instruction through hundreds of hands-on training sessions and through his books. His Flow Learning techniques, which embrace joy as part of the teaching and learning experience, have helped teachers around the world connect with their students. David Tribe, the retired Environmental Education Consultant for the New South Wales Department of Education, Australia, describes this influence: "The use of Flow Learning stages, together with the accompanying activities, makes education about the environment a joy to teach."

The essence of Flow Learning is deceptively simple. As Cornell wisely puts it, "A student's greatest assets are enthusiasm, curiosity, and a sense of wonder. If we stultify these qualities, we destroy that part in ourselves that reaches out and embraces life."

A growing body of anecdotal and research-based evidence indicates that people of any age feel happier, are physically and mentally healthier, and test better in school if they regularly play and learn in natural environments. Natural environments have a positive impact on our senses, on our spiritual health, and on our bonds with family and the larger community—including that of other species.

Simply put, as we restore our connection with nature, we restore ourselves.

Cornell's highly influential guidebook, *Sharing Nature with Children*, is elevated to a new plateau in this special, all-ages-included 35th anniversary edition. This innovative approach invites children and adults to learn about the natural world through games and other enjoyable personal connections, and presents spiritual concepts in the plain light of day. Above all, Cornell reminds us that a nature-enriched life can be a lot of fun. Educators around the world report that children dive into this experiential learning flow without realizing that their delight is all part of the plan.

In 2005, with the publication of my book *Last Child in the Woods*, I introduced the term nature-deficit disorder as a doorway into a wide societal conversation about the disconnection between people and the rest of nature, and the implications. Rising obesity rates, incidences of depression and anxiety, the surge of adult-onset diabetes strongly suggest health problems resulting from sedentary lifestyles. As the World Health Organization pointed out in a 2002 report, "A sedentary lifestyle could very well be among the 10 leading causes of death and disability in the world."*

Science doesn't have all the answers, but we do know that even limited exposure to nature can alleviate the effects of attention deficit disorder, and a little bit of contact with nature can help counter the effects of toxic stress. Correlative studies about the benefits have multiplied quickly. We

* http://www.who.int/mediacentre/news/releases/release23/en/.

need more research, but, as Howard Frumkin, dean of the University of Washington's School of Public Health says, "We know enough to act."

Now, nature-based schools are increasingly part of the conversation, and Joseph Cornell's inspirational work has influenced many of those educators, even as his writing also celebrates the importance of our urban parks, home gardens, and school grounds. As you will see, Cornell has devised ingenious nature-themed games that can be played in almost any venue. He celebrates mystery, quiet attention, observation, and the possibility of revelation. His work shines a light on values we sometimes overlook in the rush of daily life; he reminds teachers everywhere of the vital importance of a deep connection with nature.

To be sure, teachers, parents and caregivers will find practical advice for storytelling and leading nature rambles, as well as wisdom from the heart.

Many of us believe the future belongs to those nature-smart individuals who develop a deep understanding of the natural world through experiences that balance the ever-present tilt toward a virtual world. Joseph Cornell's generous and gentle work continues to offer a guiding hand.

Richard Louv is the author of Last Child in the Woods:
Saving Our Children from Nature-Deficit Disorder *and* The Nature Principle.
He is Chairman Emeritus of the Children & Nature Network.

By Tamarack Song

The guardians and scouts of traditional cultures were trained to take a two-step approach when danger threatened: first, awareness; then, action. Without the perspective that comes from full awareness of a situation, action can be misguided and ineffective.

The same is true when it comes to renewing our caring relationship with nature. There is a growing awareness of the toxic condition of our earth, and of our need for nature immersion experiences if we are to develop properly. In this twofold awareness lies hope for a future when we humans can again respectfully share the air, land, and water with the rest of life.

Fortunately, we have had our own guardians who stepped forward to raise our awareness. Sixty-five years ago, Aldo Leopold told us, in *A Sand County Almanac,* that the balance of nature is a value to hold supreme. Thirteen years after that, Rachel Carson's *Silent Spring* gave us a sobering view of what our wanton use of pesticides was wreaking.

Yet awareness amounts to nothing without action. Leopold and Carson are credited with the birth of the environmental movement and the founding of the Environmental Protection Agency.

And there was a further call to action. In Carson's 1965 essay, *A Sense of Wonder*, she encouraged parents to help their children experience the wonders of nature, which are "available to anyone who will place himself under the influence of earth, sea and sky."

Carson's call was answered in 1979 by Joseph Bharat Cornell, with the publication of *Sharing Nature with Children*. That single event marked a new level of maturity for the environmental movement, for Joseph's book clearly recognized an essential truth: the future of nature's well-being lies in the hands of our children.

Even though environmental education existed prior to *Sharing Nature with Children*, it did not answer Carson's call to bring our children "under the influence" of nature. The typical environmental education class amounted to little more than a guided tour: walk to a point of interest, listen to a talk by the naturalist, then walk to the next point of interest. It was the rare child who was taken under the influence of nature by facts and figures.

What Joseph unleashed in *Sharing Nature with Children* fomented nothing less than a revolution in environmental education. Suddenly, here was an immersion-based approach so straightforward that regular school teachers, parents, and even babysitters, could take children out and facilitate a deeply meaningful connection with nature.

Joseph's approach worked so well because it was based on a radical teaching concept—fun! Children had fun by playing the forty-two games included in the book; the games provided a means for children to revel in nature. No longer having to endure boring lectures, children were now asking questions and yearning to discover more.

Even with this great leap forward, the revolution was not over. At the same time that children were awakening, the environmental crisis was worsening.

Yet the spirit of Carson and Leopold lived on in two next-generation writers. Ten years after *Sharing Nature with Children* was published, Bill McKibben came out with *The End of Nature*, which brought us up to date on the tremendous havoc we continue to inflict upon our environment. Soon after that, Richard Louv's *Last Child in the Woods* gave a sobering assessment of how poorly we were doing with Carson's request to immerse our children in nature's wonders.

Despite the strong contribution made by *Sharing Nature with Children*, there were still many children to reach. They were suffering from what Louv called *nature deficit disorder*, stymied development caused by alienation from nature. The revolution needed reinvigorating. And for the reinvigoration to make a lasting difference, as McKibben made clear, now adults as well as children would have to be reached.

The result is the book you hold in your hand.

Built on the foundation of Cornell's first book, *Sharing Nature* reaches out not only to children, but to the inquisitive and playful child within each of us adults. The book takes us beyond our intellects, beyond our fear and despair, and into our hearts, where alone true understanding and appreciation—and true change—take place.

Joseph Cornell accomplishes this transformation through Flow Learning (see Part One of the book), which is just as radical as the fun-and-games approach that made *Sharing Nature with Children* such a groundbreaker. Much like traditional guardian training, Flow Learning takes one from awareness to action in three progressive steps: first by awakening enthusiasm; then, by focusing attention; finally, by facilitating immersion. These three steps are followed by a fourth, which has participants share with one another what has been gained. The first three steps take us from awareness to action; step four transforms what has been gained into long-term and deeply felt memories.

To know nature is to love nature—to love nature is to wish to protect nature. Flow Learning helps people know nature by getting them directly and intimately engaged. In my experience with both children and adults, hardly a person leaves a Flow Learning-guided event remaining a passive observer of nature. Nor do I remember anyone able to write the experience off as just another unmemorable event. What has touched me most deeply is witnessing adults evolving from an indifferent—or even exploitative—relationship with nature to one of caring and guardianship.

A fringe benefit of Flow Learning is that children become so engaged that boredom and the resulting discipline problems seldom occur.

I encourage you to follow Cornell's advice and adopt both the Flow Learning approach and the activities in *Sharing Nature*. In my native lifeway, intuitive tracking, and guardian training courses, I use most of the games and exercises in the book in one form or another. I modify a number of the child-oriented activities for adults, with great success. Our intuitive wisdom and intrinsic love for Mother Earth are limited neither by age nor by level of experience.

I believe Flow Learning works so well because it parallels our natural way of learning, which is an intuitive movement from observation to immersion to feeling. Because Flow Learning reflects our natural way of learning, educators I work with are able to adapt to the approach quickly and easily.

"I have a room all to myself," said Henry David Thoreau, "it is nature." Through *Sharing Nature*, Joseph Bharat Cornell uses the skill and sensitivity of a seasoned guide to show us the way to our own room. Just as Cornell walks in the footsteps of the great naturalists before him, let us walk in his footsteps and be inspired by his words for a new dawn of nature awareness: "I loved how the awakening dawn enlivened the earth—golden light flooding the fields and ponds, and birds and rabbits stirring everywhere. At sunrise, life seemed born anew; I could feel a joyous kinship with all things."

Tamarack Song is the author of Entering the Mind of the Tracker, Whispers of the Ancients, *and* Song of Trusting the Heart.
He is the director of the Teaching Drum Outdoor School.

"To create a society that truly loves
and reveres the natural world,
we must offer its citizens
life-changing experiences in nature."

~Joseph Bharat Cornell ~

Chapter One

The Story Behind
THE BOOK

I n 1971, just as I had begun my university major in nature awareness, I led my first nature walk with twenty-two second graders
from a small school in the California foothills. I had recently been
experiencing nature's sublime beauty and magnificence in the Sierra
wilderness—and I wanted the children to feel for themselves what
had moved me so deeply—a lofty goal, considering my total lack of
teaching experience.

My first mistake was heading down an old forest road without a
clear plan for how to focus the children's lively energy. Excited to be
outside and oblivious to the natural surroundings, the children used
the road as a racetrack. As they ran down the road, I hurried after
them. Eventually, we stopped for lunch, and then the students ran
exuberantly back to their classroom.

I had wanted the children to truly feel and appreciate the trees and
animals that lived around them. While I knew I hadn't achieved my
goals for the walk, I felt in my heart that there *was* a way of connecting
people deeply with nature. I just
hadn't yet found it.

Most outdoor learning at the
time used the "walk—stop—
talk" model: the leader stops at
a subject of interest, talks to the
group about it, then leads them

to the next station. The group simply listens passively. I remember going on such a forest walk in Ohio. At a certain point, I became so bored that I wondered if I was sincere in my desire to become a naturalist. Then I realized that the whole day I'd come no closer to a tree than ten yards.

In the early 1970s the idea of experiential nature activities was just starting to take off. Here I found exactly what I was seeking—nature activities helped people become fully engaged with nature, and did so in a way that exhilarated both mind and heart.

Immediately after its publication, *Sharing Nature with Children* was received enthusiastically in virtually every corner of the earth. Here, park rangers in Southern Argentina experience the Owls and Crows game during a workshop. A team of rangers spent their free evenings translating the book into Spanish for their non-English speaking colleagues.

Once I discovered how nature activities could make learning focused, dynamic, and joyful, I immediately began to create my own activities, and soon found myself having great success sharing them with others. It was heartwarming to see how children and adults playing these games became vibrantly alive, and resonated deeply with nature and with the best part of themselves.

In 1979, I published these activities in *Sharing Nature with Children*, which pioneered and popularized internationally the use of nature activities. Parents and educators across the globe were wildly enthusiastic about these games, because, as National Audubon's Vice President of Education, Duryea Morton, wrote, "by using these activities children actually experience what it is like to be a part of the natural world."

Lucy Gertz, now a manager with the Massachusetts Audubon Society, wrote in 2002 about the tremendous impact *Sharing Nature with Children* had on the field of nature education in the early 1980s:

> When a copy of *Sharing Nature with Children* landed
> in our midst, the teacher/naturalists were like vultures
> competing for the kill. Most of us were new to envi-

ronmental education. We had ecology textbooks and field guides, but little else besides what our hearts were guiding us to do. But here in this book, we found everything—philosophy, activities, and ways to lead children to meaningful environmental education experiences. This small book was hugely significant to us—it was our guide and our compass.

In almost every country today, educators, naturalists, parents, youth and religious leaders all enthusiastically use these activities. In Japan alone, over 35,000 adults have become trained Sharing Nature leaders.

I have now updated and completely rewritten that original guidebook for its 35th anniversary. Incorporated into this edition are insights that I've gained from leading hundreds of training sessions. *Sharing Nature: Nature Awareness Activities for All Ages* features the most popular and well-loved games from *Sharing Nature with Children Volumes* I & II*, as well as many new ones.

Sharing Nature with Children was published in German in 1981; in 1989 Mr. Cornell personally introduced the Sharing Nature philosophy and methods in Germany. F. W. Georg, director of the German Nature Conservancy Academy, Hessen, said,

Also included is an expanded section on Flow Learning™, the outdoor learning strategy that makes nature a joy to teach.

Each of the fifty-four activities in *Sharing Nature* has been selected for its ability to foster a deeper understanding of and rapport with nature. I wish you many splendid and memorable moments as you share the joy of nature with friends, young and old.

"Joseph Cornell has had a towering and phenomenal influence on the development of environmental education in Central Europe."

---

* *Sharing Nature with Children Volume II* was previously titled *Sharing the Joy of Nature: Nature Activities for All Ages.*

Part One

Flow Learning

Chapter Two

Learning with
THE HEART

O n a day of brilliant blue sky and white, puffy clouds, I led a group of children deep into the woods. A storm had just broken; light streaming between the clouds illumined the forest, making everything glow with life. We saw animals everywhere, exulting in the fresh vitality that follows a storm. With thirty-seven children, the group seemed large for a sensitive nature experience. But the magic of the towering, sunlit trees and brightly flowered meadows worked a spell. The children spread out spontaneously and moved through the forest in small groups. Each party of explorers made discovery after discovery; I could barely keep up with the children's urgent calls, questions, and exclamations of delight.

I remember that afternoon as a particularly satisfying experience of sharing nature with others. When we, as leaders, offer nature outings that foster sensitive discovery and direct experience, nature can change people's lives in wonderful ways.

On that particular hike, I saw such a change occur in Jack, one of the younger boys. At home Jack was a hunter—he frequently shot songbirds, thinking of them merely as challenging moving targets. That birds are living beings wasn't a reality to Jack; nor, it seemed, did he know that there were laws prohibiting the shooting of songbirds.

At the end of our hike I asked the children to lie on their backs and gaze up at the spreading branches of a large oak tree. While we were enjoying the oak from this unique perspective, we heard in the nearby trees the "tsittsit" call of a flock of bushtits—tiny, grayish-brown songbirds.

I taught the children a simple call to attract small songbirds. A flock of twenty-five bushtits responded; they flitted closer and closer through the branches until they were just a few feet above us. The bushtits' calls attracted other nearby birds. Soon western tanagers, mountain chickadees, nuthatches, and warblers were hopping about in the oak tree above us. The children were astonished by the spectacle of so many birds close by, singing and flitting from branch to branch.

Over fifty birds responded to our calls; the enthusiastic children wanted to know the name of each species. When a striking black and yellow bird with a bright red head appeared, I told them, "That's a western tanager! He's flown all the way from Mexico or Central America to raise his family in these woods." Most of the other birds stayed long enough for me to share fascinating facts about them.

The birds were so close that each one became individually alive for the children. For the rest of the week there was high interest in birds. Jack was deeply touched by the experience, and whenever we spotted a new bird he was among the first with questions about its name and habits. Jack's attitude toward birds had completely changed, and he began to appreciate them as beautiful, fellow forms of life.

Liberty Hyde Bailey, who at the turn of the twentieth century founded the nature-study movement, said, "Sensitiveness to life is the highest product of education." To encourage an attitude of respect for life, we need to begin with awareness, which leads to loving empathy. Feeling a common bond with living things makes us more concerned for the well-being of all life. The eminent Japanese conservationist Tanaka Shozo said, "The care of rivers is not a question of rivers, but of the human heart."

Mere exposure to nature isn't always enough, as a friend of mine discovered when he took his eight-year-old son hiking in the Canadian Rockies. They hiked for several hours until they came to a spectacular overlook above two glaciated valleys and several alpine lakes.

He said, "That view alone made our trip from Iowa worthwhile." He suggested to his son that they sit and enjoy the stunning mountain scenery. To my friend's dismay, the boy, who'd been running exuber-

antly back and forth along the trail, sat only for five seconds, then scrambled to his feet and started running up the trail again. My friend said he felt like screaming, "Stop! Look at this incredible view!"

We who love wild places enjoy sharing our delight with others, but, as my friend discovered, it isn't always easy to focus children's lively energies or to engage adults who have little curiosity or sense of wonder.

In the 1980s I developed a system of teaching that continues to play a central role in my work today. Thousands of educators and outdoor leaders have also found this teaching system extremely beneficial. It is a strategy that makes outdoor learning fun, dynamic, experiential, and uplifting. Since creating this system, I've been able consistently to accomplish my highest goals as a nature educator.

Because it shows how to use nature activities in a purposeful, flowing way, I call this system Flow Learning. It engages both the mind *and* the heart, where true understanding and appreciation live. It is based on universal principles of awareness and on how we learn and mature as human beings.

Flow Learning™
Natural Steps to Nature Awareness

As a young naturalist I realized there is a sequence for games and activities that, regardless of a group's age, mood, and culture, always seems to work best. People everywhere respond to this sequence because it is in harmony with deeper aspects of human nature.

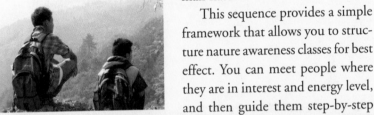

This sequence provides a simple framework that allows you to structure nature awareness classes for best effect. You can meet people where they are in interest and energy level, and then guide them step-by-step toward more meaningful and profound nature experiences.

Flow Learning's four stages flow naturally from one to the next. Each stage contains nature activities that are easy to play, joyful, intellectually stimulating, and highly engaging.

Flow Learning can be used successfully in sessions lasting from thirty minutes to all day. Although it was originally developed for teaching outdoor nature classes, it can be used to teach any subject matter, indoors or outdoors.

THE FLOW LEARNING SEQUENCE:

Stage One: **AWAKEN ENTHUSIASM**
Stage Two: **FOCUS ATTENTION**
Stage Three: **OFFER DIRECT EXPERIENCE**
Stage Four: **SHARE INSPIRATION**

Let's look at the stages one by one:

Without enthusiasm, people learn very little, and can never have a meaningful experience of nature. By enthusiasm, I don't mean jumping-up-and-down excitement, but an intense flow of personal interest and alertness.

Awaken Enthusiasm games make learning fun, instructive, and experiential—and establish a rapport between teacher, student, and subject.

Learning depends on focused attention. Enthusiasm alone isn't enough. If our thoughts are scattered, we can't be intensely aware of nature, nor of anything else. As leaders, we want to bring students' enthusiasm toward a calm focus.

Focus Attention activities help students become attentive and receptive to nature.

Stage Three: OFFER DIRECT EXPERIENCE

During immersive nature experiences, students make a deep connection with an aspect of nature. *Offer Direct Experience* activities are built on the students' enthusiasm and receptivity, and are gen-

erally quiet and profoundly meaningful.

By bringing us face to face with a bird, a wooded hill, or any natural subject, Offer Direct Experience activities give us intuitive experiences of nature.

Intuitive experiences are non-rational and provide us with inner, direct knowledge of nature. Henry David Thoreau called intuitive learning "Beautiful Knowledge."

Stage Four: SHARE INSPIRATION

Reflecting and sharing with others strengthen and clarify one's experience. Sharing brings to the surface unspoken but often universal feelings that—once communicated—allow people to feel a closer bond with the topic and with one another.

Share Inspiration activities create a sense of completion and an uplifting atmosphere conducive to embracing noble ideals.

Chapter Three

The Art of
FLOW LEARNING

As a river flows constantly toward the sea, so the essential natural direction of Flow Learning is toward greater awareness and understanding. However, just as a river varies its mood and pace—with fast riffles, placid pools, and swirling eddies—so leaders can vary the sequence of Flow Learning's four stages. As an example, because young children have short attention spans, you may want to follow a Stage Three quiet activity with a livelier Stage One game or a calming Stage Two activity. Similarly, adults and teenagers can benefit from the change of pace that a Stage One or Two game provides.

Flow Learning is designed to be fluid and responsive. During a session, one generally moves through its basic progression (1-2-3-4), but in practice, one can alter the sequence to address the immediate needs of the group. The leader, always closely monitoring the interest and attentiveness level, uses the activity appropriate to keeping the energy flowing happily and productively.

Flow Learning's third stage involves direct, intuitive experience of nature. Intuition is calm feeling, which, like a mirror, reflects life clearly. Reason can only *describe* a flowering cherry tree; it cannot help us *experience* the cherry tree.

Education is often fact driven—and cares little whether students are interested in those facts. A student's greatest assets are enthusiasm, curiosity, and a sense of wonder. If we stultify these qualities, we destroy that part in ourselves that reaches out and embraces life.

John Burroughs once said, "Knowledge without love will not stick. But if love comes first, knowledge is sure to follow. It is time enough to answer children's questions when they are interested enough to ask them." Flow Learning is learner centered—not subject driven; leaders share knowledge in ways that support and enhance deeper learning.

A major cause of teacher burnout is putting forth energy and not receiving a reciprocal response. Good teaching is a joyful exchange between student and teacher—each giving and receiving from the other.

A naturalist working at the Grand Canyon told me, "I often feel frustrated trying to share the feelings I have for the canyon with tourists, because they don't appreciate the park as much as I do. I feel I have to pull them along by my own enthusiasm, and afterwards I feel tired and drained."

While talking to the naturalist, I realized that she'd been sharing her elation for the Grand Canyon, but without helping the tourists generate the same feeling in themselves. Because Flow Learning fosters personal experience and revelation, participants rise to a high level of appreciation and inspiration. Instead of being passive learners, Flow Learners avidly and joyfully connect with both subject and leader.

On a practical level, Flow Learning helps your group get the most out of an experience by keeping the participants interested and engaged. Flow Learning can be used to teach other topics than nature awareness. Every class can benefit from students becoming more self-motivated, positive, calm, and attentive.

Chapter Four

Four Steps to
NATURE AWARENESS

Let's take an in-depth look at each stage of Flow Learning and at examples of games and activities for each one.

Stage One: AWAKEN ENTHUSIASM

Because people decide within a few minutes whether they like something or not, it's crucial to get your nature outing off to a good start. By starting with engaging (and often lively) activities, you're far more likely to win the group's wholehearted participation. If people enjoy the beginning of a class, they'll be mentally with you—and with the goals of the session.

The playful games of this stage create a strong flow of energy and interest. You have achieved the purpose of this stage when you see people come alive with joyful enthusiasm.

Enthusiasm is defined as intense and eager enjoyment and interest. Eager interest is the motor that will power your class to a worthy outcome.

Imagine sitting in a stationary car and trying to turn the front tires with the steering wheel. The resistance from the parked tires makes them difficult to turn, doesn't it? However, if you start the engine and drive as little as two miles per hour, it's easy to guide the rolling tires in the direction you want to go. Similarly, it's easier to guide students once they're in motion. Creating a sense of momentum in your class will enable you to lead your group more dynamically and fruitfully.

I call the games of Stage One **OTTER** games, because the otter is an animal that's known to play throughout its adult life. Through shared fun, the Awaken Enthusiasm  stage gives children and adults a feeling of closeness with one another. It creates a foundation of alertness and enthusiasm on which you can build subtler, more meaningful learning experiences.

The Awaken Enthusiasm games range from ones that are active and vigorous to those that stimulate and challenge one's intellectual curiosity. All the while, participants learn intriguing natural history information and develop happy associations with learning about nature.

Human nature often resists anything new. Adults and adolescents can adopt a cool, wait-and-see stance. Age-appropriate Awaken Enthusiasm games are marvelous for winning over and engaging even skeptical groups.

Wild Animal Scramble is an excellent game for encouraging passive or reserved groups to participate fully. *Wild Animal Scramble* is played by pinning a picture of an animal on each person's back, and then telling them to ask other players questions about themselves in order to find out what animal they are. Few people can resist the challenge of the game or remain coolly aloof while everyone else is chuckling at the picture of a skunk or buzzard pinned to their back. (*Wild Animal Scramble,* see page 58.)

Children usually have lots of energy. Awaken Enthusiasm games gently guide their high energy toward constructive ends. Because the children are having so much fun, these playful games deflect potential discipline problems before they arise. For adults, Stage One activities are excellent for raising energy and interest level, and for helping them re-experience the playful freedom and wonder of childhood.

The magical power of the first-stage games never ceases to amaze me. In 1986 I witnessed this power in Japan: the games worked their spell in spite of the awkwardness of speaking through a timid translator. The group of adult leaders stood with solemn faces listening politely to the translator. After a short introductory talk, I explained the *Wild Animal Scramble* game. Not knowing what to expect from this gravely courteous group, I was relieved and delighted to see every somber face break into a smile of joyful expectation. I felt the energy level of the group shoot up; the resulting spirit of lively enthusiasm lasted throughout the day.

Later, the adults watched while I worked with a group of fifteen sweet-natured second-grade girls and five ten-year-old boys. The boys were a little wild—pushing and boxing each other and producing a steady patter of smart remarks.

To establish an attitude of cooperation, I had first to capture the boys' interest. I cut short their banter by briskly hustling the children into a circle. With the circle formed and the children holding hands, I had at least an outward appearance of control. I introduced the game *Bat and Moth*, choosing the five boys to play the moths while I played the bat. As I "flew" blindfolded around the inside of the circle, I had only my "echolocation" to guide me to my prey, the moths. Every time I called out "Bat!" they had to cry "Moth!" Going toward the cry, I would try to tag the moth. The game created lots of excitement among the moths, and was tremendously entertaining for the girls. The game took about ten minutes to play; by the end, the children were having a great time and were eagerly anticipating the next game. (*Bat and Moth,* page 70.)

It is important to choose your beginning games carefully, after considering the group's age, interest, and energy level. *Wild Animal Scramble* gave the adults an amusing, energy-raising challenge that didn't compromise their dignity. Most adults and teenagers wouldn't have related to the lively, child-oriented energy of *Bat and Moth*, especially as a beginning experience. I've found, however, that older participants can enjoy active children's games once they've first been gently introduced to age-appropriate activities.

As you become familiar with the games and observe how different groups respond to them, you'll find it easy to choose the appropriate one. If the group is already reflective and eager, you may be able to touch only lightly on Stage One before moving on to a Stage Two or Three activity. On the other hand, playing an active Stage One game during a series of reflective Stage Three activities can help keep everyone's energy and interest level high.

One of Sharing Nature's core principles is that *a sense of joy should permeate the experience*. During Stage One of Flow Learning there's lots of laughter, gaiety, camaraderie, and experiential learning. Joyful play connects us with others, arouses curiosity, fosters creativity by stimulating the imagination, and helps us feel fully alive.

Flow Learning's first phase lays the foundation for its later stages, where a deeper kind of joy is experienced—the joy that comes from connecting with and belonging to the natural world.

Stage One: AWAKEN ENTHUSIASM

Quality: **Playfulness and Alertness**

- Builds on people's love of play.
- Creates an atmosphere of enthusiasm.
- A dynamic beginning gets everyone saying, "Yes, I like this!"
- Develops alertness and overcomes passivity
- Creates involvement.
- Minimizes discipline problems.
- Develops rapport between participants, leader, and subject.
- Fosters positive group bonding.
- Provides direction and structure.
- Prepares for later, more sensitive activities.

Stage Two: FOCUS ATTENTION

The human mind is a wandering mind. Years ago I demonstrated this truth to a group of twenty-five educators in Canberra, Australia. I asked each one to focus on a beautiful tree as long as possible, and to raise a hand when his attention wandered from the tree to other thoughts. After six seconds every hand was raised. The educators were astonished to see how restless their minds were.

Psychologists have reported that people generate about three hundred self-talk thoughts a minute. In 2010, two Harvard researchers, Matthew A. Killingsworth and Daniel T. Gilbert, discovered that 47 percent of the time adults think about something other than what they're doing.

To be aware of nature, one has to be attentive to nature. To observe how essential focused attention is, try the following experiment:

> Go to a wild place where the scenery is especially captivating. Gaze around you and enjoy everything you see and hear. Notice that, when you're deeply attentive, everything becomes vibrantly alive. Then observe that when your thoughts become distracted, the world of nature disappears. Continue observing the flow of your awareness—noting when you're fully present and when you're not.
>
> Imagine the power of sustained, engaged awareness. It is only by focusing our attention completely that we meet nature face to face, and truly know her.

The games in this stage give people a fun challenge that requires focused concentration for them to play effectively. As players become fully engaged in the task, they become more observant, calm, and receptive. Stage Two activities create a perfect bridge from the active, playful games to the reflective nature activities to be experienced later in Flow Learning.

The symbol for Stage Two games is the **CROW** because this bird is an extremely alert observer. You can create your own crow games by devising clever ways for people to concentrate on one of their senses.

Camouflage Trail is an excellent example of a crow game for children. To play *Camouflage Trail*, place human-made objects along a trail; have the children see how many such objects they can count. Some of the objects should be easily visible, while others (such as a rusty nail or a clothespin) should blend in with the natural surroundings.

Children and adults are unusually attentive as they walk a *Camouflage Trail*. One educator told me that she once forgot to mark the end of a *Camouflage Trail*, and her students continued walking and intently observing for an additional hundred yards before she realized what had happened and tracked them down! (*Camouflage Trail*, see page 108.)

Another favorite Stage Two activity is *Sound Map* (described on page 106). To play this game, give players a pencil and a piece of paper with an X in the center, to represent the player's location on the *Sound Map*. When a player hears a natural sound, he marks it on the map, carefully noting the sound's direction and distance. Sitting quietly, listening to the soothing voices of the nearby trees, birds, and bubbling brook, calms us and deepens our appreciation for the life around us.

The Focus Attention phase needn't last long; sometimes five to

fifteen minutes is enough.

While leading a group, it is beneficial to ask yourself the following questions:

If the group is tired and lethargic: "What Awaken Enthusiasm game would energize and lift their spirits?"

If the children are overly excited: "What Focus Attention activity would help focus and calm them?"

"How can I vary the activities and stages of Flow Learning to keep people fresh and fully engaged?"

Traditional education has focused primarily on imparting information; at least as important to consider are the energy and interest level of the students. The more students are alert, engaged, and interested, the more easily they'll both learn the information *and* experience a positive affinity for the subject.

The first two stages of Flow Learning allow you to work creatively with the mood of your group. If your group is tired, you can energize them with an active otter game; if it is too boisterous, you can quiet them with a calming crow activity.

Stage Two: FOCUS ATTENTION

Quality: Receptivity

- Increases attention span and concentration.
- Deepens awareness by focusing attention.
- Positively channels enthusiasm generated in Stage One.
- Develops observational skills.
- Calms the mind.
- Develops receptivity for more sensitive nature experiences.

Stage Three: OFFER DIRECT EXPERIENCE

The secret to knowing nature is self-forgetfulness, which comes from profound contact with the natural world. When we are completely absorbed in nature—even for a brief time—we see everything vividly. All the activities in Stage Three immerse us in nature.

Recent scientific studies have shown that contact with nature increases our feelings of aliveness, awe, and connectedness. Ecological attitudes awaken naturally during Flow Learning's experiential activities. In Germany in 2011, I conducted a two-day workshop for foresters. Afterwards, one participant told me, "As a forester, I'm used to viewing the forest as a commercial commodity. However, while doing the Sharing Nature activities, I realized that the grasses are my friends; the trees are my friends; and everything in the forest is my friend. For me, this

is a new way of looking at the forest, and it will change how I work there."

Before leading a group into an area, I look over the terrain and choose places that lend themselves to compelling, direct experiences. Then I select nature activities from the stages of Flow Learning that focus on the theme and experiences I want to convey.

Once thirty friends and I went on an outing to the California Redwoods. To help them "connect" with these magnificent trees, I set up a rope trail that led them blindfolded to many trees and fascinating nooks and crannies, all of which they explored with their hands, ears, and noses. I planned the rope trail playfully; it was full of adventurous twists and turns. The players squeezed through stands of redwood trunks growing close together, walked by a cascading stream, and passed in and out of brightly lit forest clearings.

Finally, they came to the highlight of the trail: here, it was dark and very quiet. Some thought they'd entered a cave; no longer could they hear the wind or birds singing. The ground felt hard under their feet. As they walked forward, they had to crouch, and then crawl, over a hard, polished surface. On and on they followed the rope into the unknown. Some became anxious, but I reassured them that they were safe and encouraged them to continue. They proceeded cautiously, with outstretched arms. As the opening became smaller, they could feel the rough walls around them. Several times the silence was broken by exclamations of gleeful recognition as someone in the group realized where he was. Finally, the rope led out through a small, square opening into dazzling sunlight.

We returned to the start of the trail, where they took off their blindfolds and followed the rope again to see where they had been. Those who hadn't already guessed were delighted to find that they had passed through a fallen, hollow redwood tree. They had entered at the base, then walked and crawled nearly forty feet finally to emerge through a window cut in the tree's side. They were fascinated by the tree's immense size, and spent a long time examining the tree closely.

If I had simply led my friends to the redwood tree and talked about its age, size, and natural history, they might have expressed mild interest and perhaps briefly felt it with their hands. After their personal adventure with the redwood, however, they were extremely interested, and were astonished by this towering ancient being that had long ago crashed to the forest floor.

One doesn't need to be in a wild area to provide direct experiences of nature. Most of the Stage Three activities can be played effectively in urban parks, school grounds, and backyards. Some activities can even be played indoors by using one's imagination.

The symbol for Stage Three (Offer Direct Experience) is a **BEAR**—the bear is curious, lives alone, and has the ideal temperament for communing with life. To many indigenous people, the bear is a symbol for introspection.

An excellent example of a bear activity that is easy to play and has a dramatic impact is *Camera*—played with two people: one the photographer and the other the camera. The photographer guides the camera (whose eyes are closed) on a search for beautiful and captivating pictures. The photographer takes a picture by tapping the camera's shoulder twice—the camera then opens its "shutter" (eyes) for three to five seconds. The contrast between being blind and suddenly see-ing produces the dramatic impact of the photographs. Players often report that they've remembered the image of their photographs for years afterwards.

Bird Calling, *Meet a Tree*, *Sunset Watch*, and *Mystery Animal* are just a few of the many bear activities. Each activity intensifies the player's experience of nature in a unique way. Although Focus Attention games can be similar to Offer Direct Experience activities, Stage Three activi-ties have the capacity to immerse us even more powerfully in nature.

Bear activities such as calling birds to you, meeting a special tree, walking a blind rope trail, and drawing your best view give us close interactions with the natural world. To develop a concern for the earth, we need deep, absorb-ing nature experiences; otherwise, our relation-ship with nature will remain abstract and dis-tant and will never touch us profoundly.

Stage Three: OFFER DIRECT EXPERIENCE

Quality: Communing with Nature

- Fosters deeper learning and intuitive understanding.
- Inspires wonder, empathy, and love.
- Promotes personal revelation and artistic inspiration.
- Awakens an enduring connection with some part of nature.
- Conveys a sense of wholeness and harmony.

Stage Four: **SHARE INSPIRATION**

The purpose of Stage Four is to reflect on one's experience and to share it with others. Research has shown that it isn't enough to have an experience. Reflecting on the experience clarifies and strengthens its meaning. Using the arts—such as creative writing, storytelling, poetry, and drawing—to capture and express one's experience deepens one's introspection and fosters group sharing.

Sharing brings to the surface one's individual inspiration in a way that can benefit everyone. Stage Four functions like a vast river, gathering smaller tributaries of inspiration into one dynamic flow, nourishing and uniting all river inhabitants.

Sharing also reinforces and enhances group ideals and creates an uplifting atmosphere, making it easier for leaders to share inspirational stories and ideals at a time when people are more receptive to hearing them. Stage Four activities like *The Birds of the Air* celebrate our love for nature and create a sense of completion and harmony.

DOLPHINS are gregarious, altruistic animals that cooperate with one another and appear to relate consciously with other forms of life. They beautifully express the qualities of this stage: sharing and altruism.

Sharing activities increase learning for everyone and provide feedback for the leader. You can incorporate a short sharing time in many of the Stage Two and Three activities. Varying the structure of the sharing periods keeps them fresh and interesting. For example, you can divide the group into sharing teams of three for one activity, then have an all-group sharing for the following activity.

Flow Learning's sharing phase can reveal beautiful, sometimes hidden, qualities in the participants, as I experienced firsthand in one of the most challenging classes I've ever taught. The class was comprised of thirty English teenagers from a London inner-city slum. Some of the students had fluorescent spiked hairdos. Others had safety pins stuck through their cheeks and slogans like "KILL" scrawled on the backs of their jackets.

The year was 1981. Having grown up in rural Northern California, I had never seen a group like this. I was surprised and gratified to see these challenging teenagers become avidly involved in the Flow Learning games. By the end of the session, the students were no longer displaying their tough, defiant personas. Their rebelliousness had become softened by joyful enthusiasm, calm receptivity, and feelings of interconnectedness—all fruits of the Flow Learning process.

The session ended with the teenagers expressing their appreciation and concern for the earth. Their teacher was deeply moved to see her class interacting with so much authenticity and with respect for one another.

Ending a Flow Learning session with a song or story creates closure, fosters group unity, and inspires rapport with the natural world. The tremendous power of storytelling has now been scientifically confirmed, as Peter Brown Hoffmeister writes:

> MRI scans prove stories link the brains of the storyteller and the listeners. During a story, the brain activity of all of the people involved becomes synchronized. . . .
>
> When the storyteller has activity in the insula, an emotional brain region, the listeners do too. When the frontal cortex of the storyteller lights up, so do the cortexes of all the listeners. Basically, story listeners experience the story in the exact same neurological way as the storyteller does. A story is then, literally, a shared brain experience. So when, after hearing a well-told story, a person says, "It felt like I'd been there," that's because his or her brain actually *was* there.*

---

* Peter Brown Hoffmeister, *Let Them Be Eaten by Bears* (New York: Penguin, 2013), 78–79.

Since humans began speaking, storytelling has been used to influence thoughts and behavior. Science now shows that those listening to a tale actually live the story as if it were real. Ending your outing with uplifting accounts from the lives of the great naturalists is a marvelous way to inspire a sense of idealism and altruism.

People particularly enjoy hearing tales about John Muir's meetings with wild animals and joyous wilderness adventures. To convey Muir's spirit, I wrote the book *John Muir: My Life with Nature*, which includes many easy-to-share stories.

Stage Four: SHARE INSPIRATION

Quality: Idealism

- Clarifies and strengthens personal experience.
- Increases learning.
- Builds on uplifted mood.
- Promotes positive peer reinforcement.
- Fosters group bonding.
- Encourages idealism and altruistic behavior.
- Provides feedback for the leader.

The *Joy of*
FLOW LEARNING

"The Flow Learning strategy is so potent, so gentle, that it feels like the most natural and obvious way to communicate nature education to children and adults of any age. It works in harmony with people's innate states of being, channeling their energy and contemplation at the most effective times for learning and appreciating.

"One of my favorite aspects of Flow Learning is watching a group of strangers become physically and mentally attuned to one another and to their natural environment within minutes of beginning the first stage of the program, when the Flow Learning strategy's purpose is to awaken enthusiasm. Nervousness and shyness melt away as children and adults alike adopt a playground playfulness, and the group unites in a childlike spirit of innocence, inclusivity, and fun. They are now so open and willing to learn.

"What never ceases to amaze me is that people so easily engage with Joseph's activities, and that amongst the older children in particular you can see them excited at being encouraged to play and learn and explore their senses in a way that is too often restricted to only the youngest of children. At heart, I believe people of all ages truly appreciate opportunities to return to the simplicity of the young child's world, and the Sharing Nature activities and games allow and encourage us all to do that. An unspoken permission is granted, the weight of our years is removed by the opportunity to refresh and revitalize our spirit through playing with and within our natural environment."

—Kate Akers, National Executive member,
New Zealand Association for Environmental Education

"The use of Flow Learning stages, together with the accompanying activities, makes education about the environment a joy to teach. People's faces light up with sheer joy and inner understanding."

—David Tribe, Environmental Education Consultant,
Department of Education, New South Wales, Australia

Part Two
Nature Activities

CHOOSING THE RIGHT GAME
FOR THE TIME AND PLACE

Because Sharing Nature activities are captivating and engage us directly with nature, players of all ages can happily enjoy the games together. After a family nature program in San Francisco, the parents of five-year–old Lily told the leader that their shy and hesitant daughter was uncomfortable with new situations. "When we encourage Lily to try new experiences, she usually hangs back. But while we were playing the Sharing Nature games, we were surprised and delighted to find Lily *leading us*."

In the following chapters, the activities are arranged by their Flow Learning stage. To help you easily find the best game for your group, each one has a **QUICK-REFERENCE BOX** that tells you:

*1. Awaken
Enthusiasm*

*Animal Representing
Activity Level*

CONCEPTS, SKILLS, AND
QUALITIES TAUGHT

- **When and where to play**
- **Number of people needed**
- **Suggested age range**
- **Materials needed**

*3. Offer Direct
Experience*

*2. Focus
Attention*

*4. Share
Inspiration*

For another way to find the right activity, go to Find the Best Game in Appendix B on page 194. Categories include games that work well for young children, teenagers or adults, indoors and rainy days, and science and natural history.

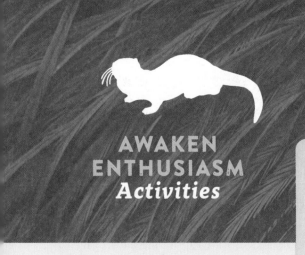

AWAKEN
ENTHUSIASM
Activities

The playful games in this section reawaken child-like enthusiasm and love for learning. They also create a joyful camaraderie within the group.

grew up near the Feather River in Northern California. When I was ten years old, I began running in the dark to greet the morning sun. I loved how the awakening dawn enlivened the earth—golden light flooding the fields and ponds, and birds and rabbits stirring everywhere. At sunrise, life seemed born anew; I could feel a joyous kinship with all things.

One of the central tenets of Sharing Nature is that a sense of joy should permeate the experience. In our workshops there are two kinds of joy—the exuberance of play and laughter, and the joy that accompanies a sense of belonging. Zestful play awakens the joyous vitality that lives within us.

Children are known for their exuberance and enthusiasm; in childhood our
brains and hearts are ideally suited for
absorbing new information and understanding. Creative play is a marvelous
medium for instilling knowledge because
it stimulates curiosity and imagination.

Because play is absorbing and liberat-
ing, adults and teenagers are rejuvenated
by periods of play that allow them to feel
again the joyous freedom of childhood.

GETTING ACQUAINTED

This lively opening activity helps participants meet and get to know one another. One player asks his partner a question; the partner then asks him one question. To encourage more interaction, tell players to ask just one question per person and not to linger long with any individual. Because the goal is to meet new people, players should seek out people they don't know. *

The Getting Acquainted Questionnaire

1. Have you ever had an exciting or inspiring experience in nature?

2. Is there an animal or plant that's especially meaningful to you?

3. What is your favorite nature activity or hobby?

4. Is there something you want to learn from nature?

5. Have you ever been lost outdoors?

6. Do you have a hero in the conservation or natural history field?

7. If stranded on a deserted island what three books would you like to have with you? Names of books: _____, _____, _____.

8. Can you recite a poem, song, or passage about nature?

9. Have you ever overcome a personal limitation while in nature?

* The Getting Acquainted activity was originally described by Cliff Knapp in his book, *Humanizing Environmental Education* (Martinsville, IN: American Camping Association, 1981).

INTRODUCTIONS
- Day and night / anywhere
- For 7 or more people
- Ages 10 and up
- One questionnaire per player, pencils

NOSES

Noses is an excellent activity for beginning a nature walk. Even while still in their chairs, players become curious and highly engaged.

Noses is a guessing game that starts with general clues that could describe many animals. As the clues progress, however, they become increasingly specific until the answer is obvious.

HOW TO PLAY: Explain that you are going to read eight clues for an animal and that players are to guess what the animal is. If someone shouts out the right answer, however, it will spoil the game for everyone else. So, players who think they know the answer should give a silent signal, by putting a finger on the tip of the nose. Tell the players, "This signal lets me and everyone else see that you know the answer."

Every clue is true, but to keep things interesting, sometimes the clues can be misleading. If you have your finger on your nose and realize you've guessed wrong, what do you do? You can cover your mistake by scratching your head or chin, and pretend your finger was never on your nose at all! (Another effective ploy is to cough gently and put your hand over your mouth.) Players enjoy covering up their nose signal in exaggerated ways, and their clowning adds to the fun.

NATURAL HISTORY
- Day and night / anywhere
- For 2 or more people
- Ages 5 and up
- Animal Clues

Tell the players: "As I read the clues, you can whisper and discuss with your neighbors what the animal might be. But don't let your voice carry across the room. Don't worry if you don't know the answer from the first couple of clues. The game is designed to keep you guessing! The animal is one everyone knows. Here are the eight clues for this animal":

1. I have two wings and lay eggs.

2. Most of us live in the tropics, but my kind is found all over the world.

3. I can fly forward, backwards, sideways, and hover in one place.

4. I'm cold-blooded.

5. I have four life stages: egg, larva, pupa, and adult. Males of my kind have bushy antennae for hearing. They can locate females by the sound of their wings.

6. I can find you by sensing your heat, moisture, and carbon dioxide.

7. Our males feed only on flower nectar, but our females feed on nectar and blood.

8. We can smell human breath seventy-five feet away. Our bites can give you malaria and many other diseases. Females of our kind lay up to two hundred eggs after every blood meal.

L N R P T H S N

To find the animal's name, write the letter that follows alphabetically in the key above. For more clues, see pages 197–200.

WILD ANIMAL SCRAMBLE

Wild Animal Scramble gets everyone instantly involved. Players learn animal characteristics and habits, and use questioning and critical thinking skills to classify their animal.

Awaken Enthusiasm games give each player a fun personal challenge, and thus ensure everyone's wholehearted participation. In this game, the players each have a picture of an animal pinned to the back of their shirts. By asking "yes or no" questions, they have to discover what animal they are. The players cannot ask questions using the names of animals or groups of animals, such as, "Am I a mammal?" or "Am I a squirrel?" Questions should be based on biological characteristics, such as, "Am I warm-blooded and do I have fur?"

According to Howard Gardner's theory of multiple intelligences, there are eight different intelligences, one of which is the "naturalist." The naturalist intelligence gives one the ability to recognize and classify natural forms such as plants, animals, or minerals.

When children first try guessing their animal, they usually don't know how to use reason to reach a conclusion. This game teaches them how to ask questions to narrow the field and classify their animal. If they receive a "yes" to the question, "Am I warm-blooded?" they know they are a mammal or a bird. If next they discover that they don't fly, they now know they are a mammal, or perhaps a non-flying bird like an ostrich. Next they might ask if they have four legs. In this simple and fun way, children become increasingly skilled at animal classification.

Wild Animal Scramble is also a group enterprise in which players avidly encourage one another. Most players feel they haven't finished the game until everyone else has guessed his or her animal. Many times I've seen six or seven players gathered around the last person, suggesting questions he could ask.

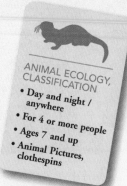

ANIMAL ECOLOGY, CLASSIFICATION
• Day and night / anywhere
• For 4 or more people
• Ages 7 and up
• Animal Pictures, clothespins

HOW TO PLAY: This game can be played with the names of animals written on index cards, but it's more fun to use pictures of animals. Postcards from nature organizations usually have a description of the animal on the back, and so enable *Wild Animal Scramble* players to verify an animal's name and characteristics.

To begin, use clothespins to attach an animal picture to each player's back. Tell the group that their questions should mention the animal's characteristics, but should not include the name of an animal or its group. Encourage each player to ask one or two questions of one other player, and then to have that other player ask a question or two in return—both players can then move on to continue with different players.

Players can respond to a question with a "Yes," "No," or "I don't know." Encourage players to use "I don't know" if they're not sure of the answer: wrong information only confuses the guessers trying to identify their animal.

Players who have guessed their animals correctly can move their animal pictures from the back to the front of their shirts.

Because the goal is for every player to be successful, the correct answer for a young child might be simply "bird," while for an experienced birder, it might be the bird's species or even subspecies.

BUILD A TREE

I created *Build a Tree* in the 1980s to help others understand how trees work. Children love this activity because it imparts tree knowledge effortlessly and kinesthetically. Besides conveying tree science experientially, *Build a Tree* evokes spontaneous laughter and a sense of camaraderie.

HOW TO PLAY: The minimum number of players needed to play *Build a Tree* is twenty. The largest number that I know of was a group of seven hundred, led by the TreePeople in Los Angeles. Actor Gregory Peck played one of the heartwoods.

Tell your group that they're going to be acting out the various parts of a tree. You will build the tree one part at a time; as you proceed, you will explain the function of each tree part. The following directions are for twenty-four players.

FOREST BIOLOGY, TEAM BUILDING
• Day and night / anywhere
• For 20 or more people
• Ages 5 and up
• No supplies

Heartwood:

To begin, choose a tall person to come forward.

Leader Narrative: "Daniel is the tree's inner core, the heartwood. He provides support for the trunk of the tree. Daniel has been around so long that he is dead, but he's well preserved. All his little pipelines are now clogged with resin."

Tell Daniel to "stand tall and support the tree."

Tree Fact: Heartwood is old sapwood (or xylem) that no longer transports water and minerals up the tree. The bulk of the tree trunk is its heartwood.

Taproot:

Next, ask a player to sit at the base of the heartwood, facing outward.

Leader Narrative: "A taproot is a long root that anchors the tree in the earth. Sally, I want you to be a taproot and plant yourself deep in the ground. Most trees don't have a deep taproot, but this one does.

"When strong winds blow, I want you to grip the earth to keep the tree from falling over. Taproots also gather water that is far underground."

Tree Fact: Most trees have shallow but widespread root systems. When trees have taproots, that root usually descends less than six feet, although the taproots of some trees grow much deeper. How far down a tree's roots grow depends on soil density and presence of water, minerals, and oxygen.

Lateral roots:

Choose three people with long hair and ask them to lie on their backs with their feet toward the heartwood and their bodies extending out from the tree.

Leader Narrative: "You are the long, shallow roots called lateral roots. A tree has hundreds and hundreds of lateral roots. They grow out from the tree like branches, but underground. Lateral roots help hold the tree upright.

"Heidi, Anna, and Kristin, please spread out your hair past the top of your head." At this point, the leader kneels beside one of the lateral roots and helps spread out her hair to demonstrate root hairs.

"Your root tips elongate and continually search for moisture. At the tips of your roots are millions of tiny root hairs that soak up water and dissolved minerals.

"I want both the lateral roots and the taproot to practice absorbing water. When I say 'Let's slurp!' all the roots make a slurping noise like this [loud drinking noise with your tongue and mouth]. Okay, let's hear you slurp!"

Tree fact: More than ninety percent of a tree's roots live within the top eighteen to twenty-four inches of soil. Lateral roots usually grow well past a tree's foliage or drip line; there's almost as much of the tree growing below ground as above.

Sapwood:

Ask three people to encircle the heartwood and hold hands. Remind players to avoid stepping on the roots!

Leader Narrative: "You are the part of the tree called sapwood or xylem. You have tiny tubes that transport water and minerals up the tree from the roots to the leaves.

"Water is called a social molecule, because water molecules stick to one another. As water molecules evaporate through holes (called stomata) in the epidermis of leaves, they draw other water molecules upward. In this way, long columns of water are drawn upward through the sapwood. On a hot day, a large tree can move one hundred gallons of water. In red oaks, water can travel at a speed of ninety-two feet per hour.

"After the roots slurp the water from the ground, your job is to bring the water up the tree. When I say 'Bring the water up!' you throw your arms upward and call out, 'Wheeee!'

"Let's practice: First the roots will slurp, then I'll tell the sapwood, 'Bring the water up!' and you'll raise your arms and call out, 'Wheeee!'"

Tree fact: On hot, sunny days, if evaporation (transpiration) is faster than the roots' ability to keep up, to prevent water loss, the tree will take a midday siesta for several hours by temporarily closing its stomata.

Cambium/Phloem:

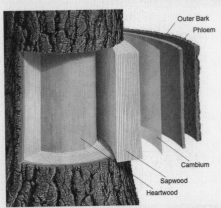

Outer Bark
Phloem
Cambium
Sapwood
Heartwood

Select six players and have them hold hands and face inward to form a circle around the sapwood.

Leader Narrative: "This ring of players represents two parts of the tree: the cambium and the phloem. On the inside of the ring is the thin cambium layer, which is the growing part of the tree. The cambium is found in the trunk, and also in the roots and branches. During the growing season the cambium makes new cells that add girth to each part of the tree.

"Trees don't grow upward from the base as does human hair. If someone nails a sign to a tree, that sign will stay at the same height year after year. A tree grows out from the middle and also outward from the tips of its roots and its branches.

"The phloem is the outer side of the cambium layer, between the cambium and the outer bark. The phloem carries the food from the leaves down to the rest of the tree.

"Let's turn our hands into leaves." Have the players in the circle stretch their arms upward and outward so that their arms cross the next person's arms at the wrist, leaving their hands free to flutter like leaves.

"When I say 'Let's make food!' raise your arms and flutter your leaves: you are making food from the sun. When I say, 'Bring the food down,' you go 'Whooo!' (As you make a long, descending whooo! sound, squat down by bending your knees and drop your arms toward the ground.)

"Let's practice two times."

Tree fact: During spring, food made in the leaves is used for new growth; during summer, extra food is stored in the roots for fall and winter. The cambium layer enables the trunk, branches, and roots to grow thicker. The phloem eventually turns into bark. The sapwood

eventually becomes heartwood. In temperate climates, different parts of a tree grow at different times of the year. Typically, a tree grows its foliage in spring, trunk in summer, and roots in fall and winter. In humid tropical rainforests, all the parts of a tree grow continually through the year.

Practice putting the parts together:

Use the tree's four-part sounds and motions in the order below. Practice the whole sequence two times.

- **Leader:** "Roots, Let's slurp."
  Roots: "Slurp."

- **Leader:** "Leaves, let's make food."
  Phloem: Flutter hands like leaves.

- **Leader:** "Sapwood, bring the water up."
  Sapwood: Raise both arms while shouting "Wheeee."

- **Leader:** "Phloem, bring the food down."
  Phloem: Squat down, bring arms down, saying "Whooo."

Bark:

Ask the remaining players to form a circle round the tree. Everyone faces outward.

Leader Narrative: "All of you are tree bark. Your thick skin keeps the tree safe from insects, disease, temperature extremes, and fire.

"To protect the tree from danger, raise your arms as would a football blocker, both elbows out and both fists close to the chest. (Pause) Can you hear that high-pitched sound, over there, in the trees? (Pause) It's the sound of the long-snouted tree-borer beetle: *Eatumupus Giganteus*. They're big, ferocious, and always hungry. I'm going to try to stop the giant beetle from coming to eat the tree, but if I fail, it's up to the bark to protect the tree."

The leader runs and hides behind a large tree. Using two sticks for antennae, he reappears as a very hungry tree-borer, scowls, and eagerly approaches the tree. The tree-borer runs or walks quickly around the tree and tries, at different points, to penetrate the bark's protective layer. The bark players try to fend off the tree-borer.

While the leader is going around the tree, he shouts the commands in sequence to lead the tree parts in their movements and sounds. Repeat the whole sequence three or four times.

- First time only: "Heartwood, stand tall and strong!" and "Get tough, Bark!"
- "Roots, let's slurp!"
- "Leaves, let's make food!"
- "Sapwood, bring the water up!"
- "Phloem, bring the food down!"

After the first round, shout the commands without giving the names of the tree part. When you finish, have the players give themselves a round of applause for being such a marvelous tree. And ask the players to help the roots up off the ground!

NATURAL PROCESSES

In this activity, players act out natural phenomena such as the life cycle of a butterfly, seasonal change, glaciation, or even the solar system. Educators can use *Natural Processes* to help students experientially learn principles taught in a previous lesson.

On an Alaskan beach, a group chose for its natural process ocean tides. The players, while holding hands, formed the shape of a crescent moon. From the crescent moon, the players expanded out and around to simulate a full moon. Leaning backwards, they turned to look at the audience, beaming brightly like a fully illumined moon.

The group then quickly formed a line and walked up the beach to stimulate a high tide. A player crouched ahead of the undulating "wave" as a barnacle and let the rising tide pass over it. The filter-feeding barnacle, previously dormant, then came to life, extending and waving its net-like feeding legs, or cirri. When the tide receded—simulated by the players walking backwards toward the ocean—the barnacle, left

UNDERSTANDING HOW NATURE WORKS

- Day and night / anywhere
- For 12 or more people
- Ages 7 and up
- No supplies

STORM

66

high and dry, withdrew its cirri and became inactive again.

Twelve to eighteen players are needed to act out a natural process. With fewer than twelve people, there may not be enough players to take all the parts; with more than twenty players, some people may not have a role. You can play *Natural Processes* with large groups by dividing them into teams. Let the groups choose a natural process, or assign one you want the teams to work on.

Some groups—especially children—may need a well-informed person to help them create their natural processes. Even for groups of adults, I make sure there's at least one nature-knowledgeable person on each team—someone who can explain the principles of the natural process, so that the team as a whole can figure out how to portray the phenomenon.

OWLS AND CROWS

Owls and Crows is an excellent game for reviewing information learned in class. To play, divide the group into two equal teams, the Owls and the Crows. Lay a rope across a clear area, and have the teams line up facing each other, each team about two feet back from the rope. About eleven feet behind each team, place a bandana on the ground to indicate home base.

When the leader makes a statement about nature, if the statement is true, the owls chase the crows; if it's false, the crows chase the owls. If a player is tagged before he crosses the home base line, he joins the opposite team.

There is a certain amount of happy pandemonium in this game—players forget which way to run or are so confused by the statement that sometimes half the players run one way, and half the other.

To minimize chaos and make things as clear as possible, use blue and red bandanas to mark the two home bases—blue, behind the crows; red, behind the owls. Tell the players that the blue bandana represents "true blue." When a statement is true, the owls chase the crows (all players run toward the blue bandana). When the statement

is false, the crows chase the owls (all players run toward the red bandana). You can also point out natural features to remind players which way to run; for example, forest for true and meadow for false.

REVIEW, NATURAL HISTORY
• Day / clearing
• For 6 or more people
• Ages 5 and up
• Rope, 2 bandanas

Make sure your clues are unambiguous and age appropriate. For example, if you say, "The sun rises in the east," students may not be sure if you mean that the sun is first seen in the eastern sky (true), or that the sun rises at all—false, because it's the rotation of the earth that makes it only appear to rise. The best statements are simple and clear: for example, "birds have teeth," or "insects have six legs and a three-part body."

Before beginning, it's helpful to make a few practice statements. Have the players point in the direction they would run instead of actually running. Once everyone can easily point out the direction for true and false statements, then begin!

BAT AND MOTH

Children love *Bat and Moth*. After playing they'll be energized and eagerly anticipating whatever is next.

Bats use echolocation, not their weak eyesight, to track flying insects. This game experientially teaches the principle of echolocation, as well as animal adaptation and predator-prey relationships, and fosters deeper listening and concentration.

Arrange the children in a circle 15–20 feet across, and ask for 3 to 4 volunteer Moths. One of the adult leaders should take the role of the Bat. To keep the game exciting for everyone, choose a bat who can move comfortably while blindfolded—he will need to be able to "fly" confidently inside the circle in order to track his prey.

To play, have the moths and blindfolded bat stand inside the circle. The bat has to tag each moth, and can use his echolocation to detect

them. To imitate sending out his natural sonar signals, the bat calls out, "Bat—Bat—Bat." To every bat call, the moths must immediately respond, "Moth." The moths can move about as long as they stay inside the circle. Gradually, the bat is able to close in on and tag one of the moths. The game is over once the bat catches all the moths.

AUDITORY
AWARENESS,
ECHOLOCATION
• Day / clearing
• For 8 or more people
• Ages 5 and up
• Blindfold

The other children stand in a circle to keep the bat and moths inside. If the bat is having a difficult time catching the moths—this game can be challenging for the bat—the leader signals each person in the circle to take a step inward to tighten the circle. If the bat continues to have difficulty, the circle may need to shrink again. The bat can also use his echolocation call

more rapidly: "Bat . . Bat . . Bat . . ," for example, instead of "Bat . . . . Bat . . . . Bat." (Wild bats increase their sonar call rate as they home in on prey.)

The children in the circle usually become excited while observing the bat hunt the moths, and may need reminders to keep quiet, so that the bat can hear the voices and footsteps of the moths.

PREDATOR-PREY

Predator-Prey has all the elements of an action movie: dramatic suspense and narrow escapes. It demonstrates food chains as well as animal behavior, and helps the players develop concentration and self-control.

In an open clearing, create a circle about 20 feet across. Ask the group to name a predator and 3 or 4 animals that are its prey, and ask for volunteers to play each animal. Tie a bell on each of these players, and have them stand inside the circle. The predator's bell should have a distinct sound—a sheep or goat bell works well. If you have a variety of bells, each type of prey animal can have a different type of bell. (Bear bells are a good choice for prey animals.)* Tie the bells on with nylon or leather string. The larger bells need to be tied on the player's thigh. Smaller bells can be tied onto the ankle or shoelaces.

* For prey animal bells, Hiker Bear Bells from Silverfoot Activewear Ltd., Squamish, BC, Canada, are highly recommended. Email: info@silverfoot.com.

Blindfold the predator and the prey animals and have them listen carefully to each animal's bell—especially to the predator's. The predator's purpose is to stalk and tag the prey animals, and the prey animals' purpose is to avoid being tagged. Prey animals can use whatever strategy seems wise: to move or to be motionless.

The players forming the circle act as boundary wardens, and whisper "circle" to any animal that starts to go outside the circle. (It's okay for the prey animals to stand just inside the circle.) To help the predator locate the sounds of his prey, tell the players forming the boundary circle to remain quiet. As in *Bat and Moth*, if the predator is having difficulty capturing his prey, ask the players in the circle to take a large step inward to narrow the circle. To keep the game interesting for all, choose the person acting as the predator for qualities of confidence, poise, and energy.

ADAPTATION,
FOOD CHAIN,
PREDATION

- Day / clearing
- For 10 or more people
- Ages 8 and up
- Bells, blindfold

PYRAMID OF LIFE

Pyramid of Life demonstrates food chains and other ecological concepts in a lively, experiential way. To prepare, write on cards the names of plants, plant-eaters, predators, and one top, or apex, predator; number each card with its trophic level (plants, I; plant-eaters, II; primary predators, III; and top predator, IV).

Because plants and animals form an interconnected community, choose subjects from a local habitat or ecosystem, such as freshwater, grassland, or ocean. For example, for a class of twenty-seven participants, select fifteen plants, seven herbivores, four predators, and one apex predator. (In the accompanying sidebar are twenty-seven fun plant and animal names to use until you can create your own set.)

Give each player a card. Then ask players with a I on their card to come forward, form a line facing the rest of the group, and introduce themselves. You can then ask, Are you all plants? Yes, they reply. Ask the plants to kneel in a line facing you.

Then ask those with II on their cards to come forward and introduce themselves. Are you all plant-eaters? Yes. Please line up (standing) right behind the plants. III: predators? Yes. Please line up behind the plant-eaters.

Now there is only one person left. Ask if anyone has a IV. When that player comes forward and introduces himself, tell him he is the top of the food chain, and have him stand behind the third row.

Explain that each stage of the food chain is called a trophic level. As life ascends the food chain from one trophic level to the next, each level retains only

FOOD CHAINS, BIOLOGICAL MAGNIFICATION
• Day / clearing
• For 6 or more people
• Ages 7 and up
• Pencils & paper, plant and animal cards

ten percent of the biomass of the previous level. That is, a thousand pounds of plant biomass supports a hundred pounds of herbivore, which in turn supports ten pounds of carnivore, which supports one pound of apex predator.

Ask the kneeling plants, "If we built a human pyramid to represent the food chain, could you support all the animals behind you?" NOOOO!!! "Well, we're not going to build a pyramid today, so you can relax!"

Explain that you will, however, use the trophic levels to demonstrate how pesticides concentrate as they move up the food chain. The toxins in pesticides remain in the tissue of whatever life is exposed. When that life form is eaten by one higher up the food chain, the pesticide also is absorbed. The higher in the food chain, the greater the concentration of pesticide.

Tell the first row, "The plants don't look very good. I see that insects have been eating you. To help protect you, I'm going to spray you with pesticide. Don't worry, it won't hurt! The bandana represents one poison part of pesticide." Then place a bandana on the head of each plant.

Now ask the second row to gather the bandanas from the plants and put them on their own heads as if they had just eaten the plants. Then have the primary predators (third row) take the bandanas from the herbivores and place the bandanas on their heads. Finally, the apex predator gathers all the bandanas and piles them on his head.

Tell the group, "The golden eagle, which consumes a large variety of herbivores and predators, inherits ALL of the pesticide. Golden eagle, could you now keel over and succumb to pesticide poisoning?"

Explain that the scientific name for the increasing concentration of toxic chemicals in the tissues of organisms at higher levels in a food chain is "biological magnification." Banning DDT and other pesticides has increased the populations of apex predators, such as the peregrine falcon and the brown pelican.

To conclude the activity, you could ask, "Where do most human beings eat on the food chain?"

Fun plant and animal names for
PYRAMID OF LIFE

I Plants
- prairie rose
- touch-me-not
- northern lady fern
- common horsetail
- bleeding heart
- pignut hickory
- sugar pine
- baby blue eyes
- monkey flower
- dogwood
- old-man cactus
- poison oak
- Virginia spring beauty
- black-eyed Susan
- locoweed

II Herbivores
- leaf miner
- shining flower beetle
- Clark's nutcracker
- dusky-footed wood rat
- eight-spotted forester (moth)
- yellow-bellied marmot
- right-handed pond snail

III Primary Predators
- hairytail mole
- hognose snake
- short-tailed weasel
- red-bellied woodpecker

IV Apex Predator
- golden eagle

SLED DOGS

Sled Dogs is excellent to use with adults and adolescents to demonstrate principles of leadership and cooperation.

In snow country, sled dogs are noted for their tremendous enthusiasm for running and pulling heavy loads. Yet, just as with humans, not all sled dogs are alike. The secret of a successful sled dog team is taking advantage of the strengths of each dog. Some dogs are strong, but don't listen very well. Other dogs listen well but haven't much confidence.

Strong dogs who don't listen well but are powerful are placed close to the sled, where they can do good hard work, and follow the other dogs.

The dogs in front of them are team dogs. They, too, do best following other dogs; they provide the "horsepower" to move the sled. Some dogs enjoy the mental challenge of being the lead dog. The musher, or driver, depends on his lead dog to listen for and follow his commands, and to make instant decisions when necessary. Lead dogs must be both intelligent and strong to keep the team moving fast.

The lead dog, however, would be unable to turn the rest of the team without the help of the swing dogs. These dogs run immediately behind the leader; they help him keep the fast pace and aid him in getting the team to turn when necessary.

Another essential in a successful team is for each dog to participate fully. Occasionally a dog will run with the team but not pull any of the weight—he is betrayed by his slack tug line (the line that ties him to the main tow line).

COOPERATION, LEADERSHIP
- Day and night / anywhere
- For 8 people (plus audience)
- Ages 13 and up
- Rope (15 ft. long), winter hat, scarf, chair (on casters)

The parallels to human beings are obvious. In any group endeavor, many different roles must be fulfilled. Each role is important to the success of the enterprise. Each person should be respected for his strengths; a leader should try to place individuals where they will fit best and contribute most. The goal is that each person be able to use his strengths to the utmost, and in doing so pull his full share of the weight. Not everyone can be, or wants to be, a leader, but each person has something essential he can offer to the whole.

HOW TO PLAY: Tie a strong, fifteen-foot piece of rope to the back of an office chair on casters. The chair will be the sled and the rope the towline. (You can tie a loop in the rope for each dog to make it easier for them to pull the sled.) Choose someone to be the musher and have him kneel on the chair, facing the backrest (and the towline). The musher's name is Pierre. Have Pierre wear the winter scarf and hat.

Call out two people to be the strong dogs and place them in front of the sled; one dog on each side of the rope. Strong dogs have lots of energy, but don't follow directions well. The names of these dogs are Rocky and Daisy.

Pick two more participants to be the team dogs. Place them in front of the strong dogs. These dogs are good followers and provide horsepower for the sled team. Their names are Molly and Buddy.

Next choose two players to be the swing dogs. These dogs help keep the fast pace and aid the leader in turning the sled team. Place the swing dogs in front of the team dogs. Their names are Princess and Duke.

Finally, select one person to be the lead dog. This dog is intelligent, listens well, follows directions, and makes good decisions. The lead dog's name is Missy. This dog is a fast runner and stretches the towline so that the other dogs won't get tangled up with one another.

Now that you have introduced the team roles, have your group ask themselves, "If I were a sled dog, where would my strengths and temperament place me?" and, "In the way that swing dogs support a fast pace and aid in turning the sled, do I actively support the goals of my group?"

To end the activity, have the sled dogs pull Pierre around the room or pavement.

Sled Team Members:

Musher: Pierre
Strong dogs: Rocky & Daisy
Team dogs: Molly & Buddy
Swing dogs: Princess & Duke
Lead dog: Missy

ANIMAL PARTS

Animal Parts promotes group creativity and works beautifully with either children alone or families.

Divide your group into teams of four or five people. Ask each group to choose an interesting or favorite animal. Once they've made their choice, tell the teams that each team has to use all its members to form the head, body, and limbs of their chosen animal.

Have the teams go off on their own to create their animal and practice its movements and behavior so that the audience will be able to recognize who they are. Encourage the teams to rely on how the animal moves and behaves rather than on its distinctive calls. Give the groups five to ten minutes to work on their performances.

How to make the parts of an animal? Several team members could represent legs or wings—one member for each. Someone else might be the tail. The kangaroo could hold a small child in her pouch. One person could use hands and sticks to become the antlers on the head of a male deer. A red sweater could be used on the head of a red-headed woodpecker.

ANIMAL CHARACTERISTICS, MOVEMENT, AND BEHAVIOR

- Day and night / anywhere
- For 3–6 people in a group
- Ages 5 and up
- No supplies

Once all the groups are ready, have them come forward to the "stage," one group at a time, to present their animals. Ask the audience to wait until the group has completely finished its performance before shouting out their guesses.

ANIMAL CLUE GAME

Animal Clue Game joyfully captures the group's attention by making learning fun, creative, and engaging. Camaraderie is quickly created among milling players as they discover fascinating animal facts and characteristics.

First, create your clue cards. Choose five animals from a specific ecosystem such as marsh or grassland. The animals should be diverse in characteristics. Create six clues to describe each animal, to give you a total of thirty clues.

Here are sample clues for one animal. Can you guess what it is? (*See the bottom of the next page for the answer.*)

- I can hear and talk with others of my kind over distances up to thirty-five miles.
- I breathe through two holes in the top of my head.
- As a baby I weigh seven tons.
- My body has a very thick layer of blubber.
- I eat about three tons of krill every day.
- I'm the largest creature that ever lived on Earth.

You can use the Ocean Animal clues from *Sharing Nature Online Resources* or you can create your own clues. You will need thirty small cards. Write one clue on each card. For more than thirty players, you can use more animals.

HOW TO PLAY: Each player is given one or two animal clue cards. The group needs to work together to identify the five animals and collect all six clues specific to each animal.

ANIMAL TRAITS, CLASSIFICATION
- Day and night / anywhere
- For 5–30 people
- Ages 9 and up
- Clue cards

81

After the starting signal, players immediately begin sharing their clue cards and calling out the names of animals they think their clue cards describe. For example, a player's card might say, "I am warm-blooded and have a long tail and four feet." The player thinks, "Maybe I'm a squirrel," so he calls out, "Squirrel! Squirrel!" No one else is shouting, "Squirrel," or responding to his call. But someone *is* calling, "Otter," and the player notices several other people heading in the otter-person's direction. He checks his clue again and realizes he could be an otter, so he joins the group trying to collect all the otter clues.

The leader mingles with the group and gives help as needed, but for the most part lets the players figure things out among themselves. Children who can't read well or who are unfamiliar with the animals can be given the easiest clues.

When the members of a group think they've collected all six clues for one animal, give them a master clue list for that animal as a way to check their answers. After all the animals have been identified and the correct clue cards collected, have members of each group read aloud two of their most interesting clues.

(*Answer to clues on page 81: Whale or Blue Whale.*)

Tips for making your own cards for the ANIMAL CLUE GAME

- It's important to choose animals whose characteristics set them apart from the other animals on your list.

- For example, one wouldn't confuse clues for a bear with clues for a snake, but clues for a bear and clues for a raccoon would be harder for children to distinguish. Selecting distinctive animals also makes it easier for you to write your clues.

- Adapt *Animal Clue Game* for preschoolers by making puzzle pieces from a photograph or drawing of an animal. Cut three or four puzzle-piece clues per animal. For example, from a duck picture, cut out pieces showing the duck's webbed feet, head and bill, and body.

- A calmer, more comprehensive way to play *Animal Clue Game* is to give the thirty clue cards to a team of four or five players. The players work together to find the five animals and their correct clues. In this version, players are able to read and discuss all thirty clues intently.

- To enable the players to check their answers, place—face down—pictures of the animals and a clue list for each team.

ANIMAL
CLUE RELAY

Animal Clue Relay is similar to the *Animal Clue Game*, but the "relay" aspect helps generate a tremendous excitement among players—in a disciplined, manageable way. Because this game awakens enthusiasm and fosters cooperation, it's a perfect activity to start the day, to use after lunch, or to use when you need to perk up the energy in the late afternoon. After playing this game, the group is energized and eager for whatever comes next.

This active version of *Animal Clue Game* also uses the thirty-card set. In this version, however, players have only to discover the five different animals, not to collect or remember the six clues for each animal.

Have the players divide into teams of three or four, and give a pencil and notepad to each team. (To add to the fun, each team can choose an animal name for itself. Before playing, go around the circle and have each team introduce itself by shouting its name.)

Place all thirty clues face up in the center. Have the teams spread out so that each team is about ten feet from the clues.

At the starting signal, each team sends one runner into the center of the circle to get one clue card (without looking at it) and bring it back to the team. All the teammates read the clue together. If someone thinks he or she knows the animal, a teammate writes its name on the paper. Then another runner returns that clue card and gets a new one. During the game, teams try to read as many clues as they can in order to identity all five animals. When teams feel confident they know all five animals, they can bring their list to the leader.

To make the game flow faster, I suggest the following:

- If there are eight or fewer teams, each runner brings back two cards instead of just one.

- After the team has gathered a few clues, the runner scans each new clue card before bringing it to his team, to make sure his team hasn't already read it.

Animal Clue Relay works well for family groups, too, even when children cannot read. Young children are excited to run and pick the clues, and adults are happy to let them. When a little boy returns with *his* clue, he'll listen intently as his mother reads it aloud, and he'll eagerly make his own guesses.

NOAH'S ARK

Imagine it's mid-afternoon and interest is flagging. *Noah's Ark* can save the day. This quick and simple game revives sagging spirits through joyous play. Play that is energizing and engrossing frees people from passing moods and discomfort.

In this game, players are given the name of an animal, then asked to make the movements, behavior, and sounds of the animal, in order to attract another individual of its kind. For example, a player given "penguin" might bray and waddle with his arms held tight by his side, as he looks for another penguin in the group.

When told to act like their assigned animal, players are at first self-conscious. But, surrounded by other players in the same situation, they happily enter into the spirit of the game.

HOW TO PLAY: Beforehand, create a list of animals that are distinctive, fun, and familiar. Number the list.

Have the group form a large circle. Count the number of players and divide the total in half to determine how many animal pairs you will need. If you have an odd number of players, you can designate three players for one of the animals.

Go around the circle with the numbered animal list, and secretly show each player his or her animal. If there are thirty players, for example, give players one through fifteen each an animal; give player sixteen the same animal as player one, player seventeen the same animal as player two, and so on. (Or, if you prefer, you can create two cards for each animal and give a card to each player.)

Then tell the group the following:

"Noah was one of the world's first conservationists. We are told that before the big flood, he gathered two of every creature and put them into his ark. It's because of Noah that we have wildlife today. This game, *Noah's Ark*, reenacts Noah's gathering of two of every kind of animal for his ark.

"The animals can help Noah by forming into pairs. To distinguish itself from the other animals, each animal will act out the mannerisms, behavior, and calls unique to its species."

Have the players turn and face the outside of the circle. Ask them to close their eyes and imagine themselves in their animal's native habitat. By aping their animal with gentle body movements and quiet sounds, players begin *becoming* their animals. When the players are ready, ask them to face inside the circle and search for their mate.

Immediately, the animals come to life—in a clamor of braying, croaking, jumping, and slithering—each animal trying to attract its partner. As, one by one, the pairs recognize each other, happy laughter breaks out and the united pairs proceed to the ark, to be welcomed by Noah.

GUESS AND RUN!

Guess and Run!, with its drama and chase, makes learning about animals exciting as well as instructive. Because the game can be played outdoors and indoors, it's a good rainy day activity. After the children play *Guess and Run!*, they're eager to read field guides and search online to discover interesting animal facts for the next round.

Divide the players into two equal teams of up to eight players each. Give each team a pencil and notepad, and have the teams choose an animal that is familiar, but that the other team might not think of immediately.

Each team writes down six to eight clues for its animal. The first clues are general—clues that could describe any number of animals. For example: "I live in the forest" or, "I have a lot of character for a guy without a backbone."

The final clue should be so specific that the other team will definitely know what animal it is: "I have a small black body, a bushy tail, and a long white stripe down my back and tail. I can spray a foul-smelling oily liquid to keep predators away." (See *Noses* on page 56 for an example of eight animal clues going from general to specific. More clues can be found on pages 197–200.)

The clues should tell interesting facts about the animal, and become increasingly specific from the first general clue to the final, give-it-away clue.

ANIMAL CLASSIFICATION, ANIMAL FACTS
- Day / clearing or road
- For 4–16 players
- Ages 7 and up
- Rope, pencils, paper, 2 bandanas

TO PLAY THE GAME: Place a rope between the two teams, with one team, the Guessers, standing next to the rope, and the other, the Clue Givers, standing 2 feet away from the rope. Place a bandana about 11 feet away on each side of the rope to indicate each team's home base line. (Runners don't have to tag or stand on the bandana itself—they just have to run past the eleven-foot line before being tagged. Be sure to check the running area for hazards.)

The Clue Givers appoint one person to read the clues. As the first clue is read, anyone on the opposite team can call out a guess. One of the fun challenges of the game: Only the first guess counts. And no one on the Clue Givers team can run back to home base until the team's reader says, "Yes."

Once the clue is read, the reader listens for the *first* guess from the Guessers, and responds (probably), "No." Any guess after the first one, even if correct, doesn't count. As the clues become more obvious, the tension builds and everyone gets ready to run!

Because of the excitement and the desire to avoid being tagged, the Clue Givers sometimes bolt before the reader says "yes." (Be sure to choose a reader who can confidently call out a loud "yes" or "no." And, of course, one who won't bolt for home base before answering "yes"!)

To help the players learn to heed this rule, you can penalize any player who runs too soon by replaying that last clue. Bring everyone back to the rope and have the reader give the same clue again; this time the early runners have to stand straddling the rope, thus giving the opposite team a better chance of tagging them. The players quickly learn to wait for the "Yes."

After one team's animal has been guessed, the other team has its turn.

GUESS AND RUN! *Version II*

The children line up on one side of the rope, and the leader(s) on the other side. The leader reads the clues one at a time; the children guess after each clue. When they guess correctly, the leader calls out "Yes," and the children try to tag the leader before he can run past his goal line. In this version, the opportunity to chase the leader brings special glee to the children.

FOCUS
ATTENTION
Activities

The games in this section help us become better observers of nature.

As a young boy, George Washington Carver, the renowned botanist, was a keen observer of nature. For his remarkable ability to sense exactly what was wrong with a plant and prescribe a cure, he was known in his town as "the plant doctor." People were astonished by young Carver's knowledge, especially since—a freed slave—he'd never been to school.

To little George Carver, his gift was very simple. When people expressed amazement over his rapport with plants, he would say, "People just *look* at their flowers. They don't *see* them like I do." By carefully observing a plant, he could see exactly what it needed.

I AM CURIOUS ABOUT

*"I roamed the countryside searching
for answers to things I did not understand.
Why shells exist on the tops of mountains. . . .
And how a bird suspends itself in the air."*
—Leonardo da Vinci

Curiosity is one of the most important human qualities because it opens us to new worlds, knowledge, and opportunities. The inquisitiveness and wonder of childhood should be encouraged throughout one's life.

Curiosity, or avid interest, fosters creativity and innovation. When we're curious, we see things with fresh—not tired—eyes, and we become aware of the nuances of life. Suspending judgment and preconceptions helps us see things in the present moment, as they actually are. We discover the unfamiliar in the familiar.

HOW TO PLAY: Go to a natural area and look for something you're curious about. Write your question on a piece of paper. You might ask yourself, for example, "Why do some insects have translucent wings?" or, "Why does this species of pine tree have large cones?" After closely observing your subject, think of several possible answers to your question.

It's not important that your guesses be accurate. The time you spend pondering your subject will help you establish a stronger rapport with it.

Have fun. Be imaginative and creative. See how many different answers you can create. *Exercise* your curiosity!

SENSE OF WONDER,
OBSERVATION

- Day / anywhere
- For 2 or more people
- Ages 5 and up
- Pencils, paper

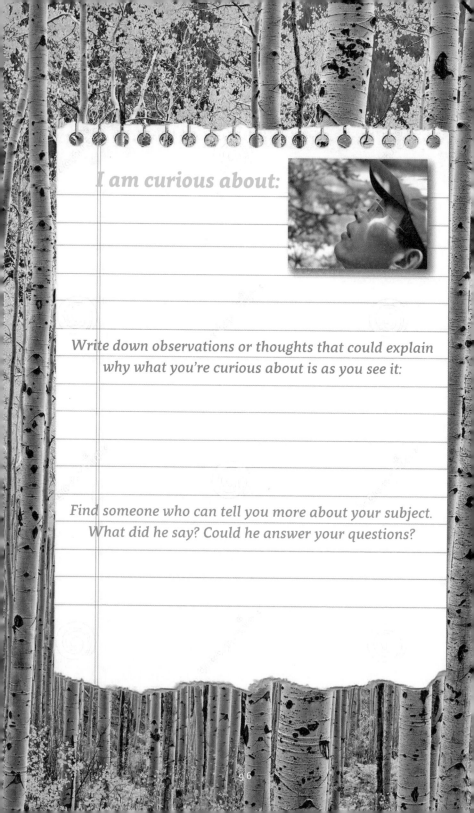

I am curious about:

Write down observations or thoughts that could explain why what you're curious about is as you see it:

Find someone who can tell you more about your subject. What did he say? Could he answer your questions?

SOUNDS AND COLORS

My friend Renata shared a heartwarming story about the *Sounds* game. Her seventy-three-year-old Lithuanian grandmother, Mary, has Alzheimer's and is now always anxious and restless. It's difficult to find any activity, even walking in nature, that helps her calm her anxiety.

Nonetheless, during a visit, Renata took Mary into the backyard garden. Remembering the simplicity of the *Sounds* game, Renata asked Mary to close her eyes and listen to the noises around her. "Grandma," she asked, "can you count the different sounds you hear?"

For eight minutes, Grandma listened attentively to the sounds around her, raising her fingers at each different sound. Then, opening her eyes, she began carefully listing each sound she'd heard: bird, car, people talking, wind in the leaves, her granddaughter breathing, and an insect flying by.

After just a few minutes of playing the *Sounds* game, to Renata's amazement, Mary was transformed. Now she was calm and focused, and her face was shining with joy. For nearly an hour afterwards, Mary's calmness remained.

"To perceive freshly, with fresh senses, is to be inspired . . . the age of miracles is [in] each moment." (Thoreau) The simplicity of the *Sounds* game makes it easy for children and adults to connect directly with the natural world.

SOUNDS

Why is the young boy sitting quietly and so absorbed? He's listening intently to the sounds around him. Each time he hears a bird singing in the forest— a bumblebee buzzing—or dry grass swishing in the wind—he indicates it by raising a finger.

To play *Sounds*, ask children to sit with their elbows bent and fists closed at shoulder level facing forward. Each time they hear a new sound, they lift one more finger. Challenge children by asking, "Can you hear ten different sounds?" Having children close their eyes will help them concentrate better.

AUDITORY AWARENESS
• Day / anywhere
• For 1 person or more
• Ages 3 years and up
• No supplies

If you are playing in a noisy city park, have the children listen only to natural sounds.

COLORS

Colors challenges children to see how many different colors and shades of color they can count as they stand in one place.

For example, you could ask, "How many shades of green can you see?" After the children respond, tell them, "Green is one of nature's favorite colors. Most plants are green because they contain the chemical chlorophyll, which allows them to absorb energy from the sun. Plants differ in how green they look because they have different amounts of chlorophyll pigment in their leaves." (Plants also have other pigments that affect their color.)

If you are on a cliff overlooking the ocean, you could ask, "How many colors can you see in the water below?"

VISUAL
AWARENESS
• Day / anywhere
• For 1 person or more
• Ages 4 years and up
• No supplies

Light changes color. Every twenty-four hours we witness the blackness of night transition into a feast of brilliant daytime color. In the Grand Canyon, because of changing light, the rocks seem alive as they turn color from moment to moment.

Ask children to observe a natural scene and watch how the changing play of light alters the color and mood.

I CAN SEE

I Can See helps children and adults become more mindful and immersed in their natural surroundings. Even though this activity is played for just a few minutes, its simplicity can bring people powerfully into the present moment. During a workshop I gave in North Carolina, a Duke University student who felt overwhelmed by her upcoming final exams practiced *I Can See*. After the experience, she told me, "Immediately I became aware of the world around me: I *saw* the nearby trees and *heard* the sounds of the forest. I totally forgot about my exams and feel less anxious now."

Thoreau said, "The age of miracles is [in] each moment." This simple activity grounds us in the here and now, and enables us to discover life's beauty and richness.

HOW TO PLAY: Divide into groups of two and have each pair find a captivating place in nature. Once there, one of the players sits or stands behind the other. The person sitting behind is the Coach and the one sitting in front is the Player.

AWARENESS OF LIFE
• Day / anywhere
• For 2 or more people
• Ages 10 and up
• No supplies

The coach begins by saying, "I can see." The player then says the first thing he sees, for example . . . "the tall trees." The coach continues prompting the partner by repeating other simple phrases. After each one, the player replies with an observation, as in the following example:

Coach: "I can hear . . ."
Player: "the tap-tap of a woodpecker."
Coach: "I can smell . . ."

Player: "the flowering bush."

Coach: "I can feel . . ."

Player: "the peace of the forest."

The coach can repeat the phrases multiple times, and can also create personal phrases. The teams play as long as they have interest (usually about three minutes), then the players can switch places and roles.

A more reflective version of this activity, *I Am the Mountain*, can be found in my book, *The Sky and Earth Touched Me: Sharing Nature Wellness Exercises*.

To play I CAN SEE *with several children:*

Have the children sit close together in a line in front of you. Tell the children that you will prompt each child with a phrase, starting with the child on the left. I like to vary my prompts; for example, for the first child, say, "I can see"; for the second child, "I can hear." Continue to go down the line of children several times until each child has answered three or four times. Make sure each child has had the opportunity to answer a hearing, smelling, and feeling statement.

HOW CLOSE?

The naturalist Enos Mills stood on the Continental Divide at twelve thousand feet. He had lost his snow glasses, and the intense sunlight reflecting off the snow soon blinded him. His sunburned eyes swelled shut.

Blind and alone on top of the Rocky Mountains, the nearest house miles away, Mills needed to move carefully. He felt his way with his feet and staff, trying to avoid stepping off a cliff or into a steep canyon. He shouted for help but no one answered. He listened intently, however, to the echoing answer after each shout, noting its direction, intensity, and cross echoes. Mills concluded that he was going down into a deep, forested canyon.

For the best chance of finding other people, he needed to walk eastward. To make sure he was traveling east, he climbed out of the canyon and felt the trees on the upward slope to his right, noting that most of them were Engelmann spruce, which inhabit north-facing slopes. To be doubly sure, he climbed up the slope to his left and discovered that most of the trees were Limber pines, which grow on south-facing slopes. Mills now *knew* he was heading east

After a cold night of careful walking, Mills felt the morning sun. Loss of his sight allowed his other senses to offer him a wealth of impressions. His ears caught the chirps of birds and the soft plunk of icicles falling in the snow. When a cloud passed overhead, he could estimate its size by feeling how long its passing shadow blocked the warmth of the sun. He

constantly analyzed the air. At one point he smelled wood smoke, but the swirling air currents disguised its direction.

Late in the day, his nose detected the odor of an old corral. Adjoining the corral he found a cabin. After two strenuous days and one night, he was exhausted, lay down on the cabin floor, and fell quickly asleep. When Mills awoke, his limbs and legs were so cold that more than an hour passed before he could stop shivering and walk.

He found a road where he could stroll at a normal pace. Soon he detected the pungent smell of burning aspen and knew he was close to human habitation. Not wanting to pass it by, he stopped to listen.

Then he heard a little girl asking gently, "Mr. Mills, are you going to stay with us tonight?*

HOW CLOSE?

While walking outdoors, children and adults often pay little attention to their environment. Players of *How Close?* experience in a dramatic way the importance of being aware of one's surroundings. Participants learn to be especially attentive to the direction of the wind, the slope of the land, the location of the sun, microclimates, pungent smells, the calls of birds and other natural sounds.

AWARENESS, ORIENTEERING
- Day / open field
- For 3 or more people
- Ages 8 and up
- Bandana, blindfolds

Not only does *How Close?* help people become better nature observers, it can also help save lives. Hikers often become lost or temporarily disorientated while navigating dense forests or other confusing terrain. Thick fog, snowstorms, and failing light can also cause hikers to lose their bearings.

* A rewritten account of "Snow-Blinded on the Summit" from *Adventures of a Nature Guide* by Enos Mills (1870–1922).

In *How Close?* blindfolded players use their senses of touch, hearing, and smell to discover environmental clues to help them safely navigate across an open field or meadow.

HOW TO PLAY: Find a large open meadow or field where it is safe to walk. If possible, look for a meadow with small hills or sloping ground, to add variety to the landscape. Have the players form teams of two. One player is the Guide. The other player is the Walker, who'll be blindfolded (or will keep his eyes closed).

The players stand in a line, and the leader walks 67 steps (or about 1/30 of a mile) away from them across the open meadow. When the leader is ready, he waves a flag or bandana at the group. All the walkers look at the position of the leader. Then they close their eyes or put the blindfold over their eyes. The blindfolded players try to walk in a straight line toward, and end up as close as possible to, the leader.

The guide goes along to make sure the walker is safe. The guide does not influence the walker in any way unless he is about to walk into something hazardous. When the walker comes even with the leader, the guide taps the walker's shoulder to signal "stop." As each walker approaches the leader, the leader holds his arms out to the sides to create an imaginary line, so that the guide knows when the walker has reached the destination line.

Before the first group of players start walking, ask the group, "What natural phenomena (such as wind, sun, slope, and bird calls) might help you stay on a straight course?" Tell the players who have finished to remain quiet so that they won't influence the players still walking.

Players of *How Close?* are amazed how challenging it is to walk in a straight line. Few can do so. I've noticed that after the game is over, participants are much more humble and observant, and keen to learn orienteering skills.

How Far Off the Mark Were You?

After the walkers have reached the imaginary line, it is instructive to estimate how far from the destination point (leader) they would have been if they'd traveled not 1/30th of a mile, but a full mile. Players are keenly interested in finding out if they can walk in a straight line, and in knowing how far off the mark they would have been had they

kept walking for a mile: Many discover they would have missed the leader by as much as five miles!

In order to know how many steps equal 1/30 of a mile, the leader needs to measure his length of stride. For example, the length of my stride is 31.5 inches. Below is how I determined how many of my strides equal 1/30 of a mile:

- In a mile there are 5,280 feet, which equals 63,360 inches.
- 63,360 divided by 30 gives the number of inches in 1/30 of a mile: 2,112 inches.
- I then divided 2,112 inches by 31.5 inches (my step) to find out how many steps of mine equal 1/30 of a mile.
- The answer is 67 steps.

When all the walkers have reached the imaginary line (where the leader is standing), have them walk without blindfolds to the leader, counting how many strides away they were, making each step approximately a yard in length. Multiply the steps by 3 to get the number of feet, then multiply that number by 30. The total number of feet is the distance by which you would have missed the destination if you had walked a mile.

For example, if you counted 20 strides to the leader, you would multiply 20 strides by 3 feet to equal 60 feet. You would then multiply 30 by 60 to equal 1,800 feet. You would have been off the mark by 1,800 feet—about 1/3 of a mile.

SOUND MAP

The drumming of a wood-pecker—wind streaming through the trees—flutelike calls of a hermit thrush—water cascading down a steep, rocky incline.

Enchanting choruses of natural sounds delight players of *Sound Map*. Children love this activity and sit surprisingly still while mapping the sounds around them.

To play, give each person a piece of paper with an X marked in the center. Tell the participants that the paper is a sound map and that the X represents where each player is sitting (once he's chosen his spot). When a player hears a sound, he makes a mark on the paper to represent the sound. The location of the mark should indicate the direction and distance of the sound from the player's seat. Tell players not to draw a detailed picture for each sound, but to make just a simple mark. For example, a few wavy lines could represent a gust of wind, or a musical note could indicate a singing bird. Making simple marks keeps the focus on listening rather than on drawing.

Encourage the players to close their eyes while listening for sounds. To help them increase their hearing ability, ask them to make "fox" ears by cupping their hands behind the ears. This hand position will create a greater surface area to capture sounds. Then show them how to cup the hands in front of the ears (palms facing backwards) to hear sounds behind them more easily.

AUDITORY
AWARENESS,
ORIENTEERING

• Day and night /
  natural area
• For 1 person or more
• Ages 5 and up
• Paper, pencil(s)

To hear a variety of natural sounds, choose an area that encompasses several habitats, such as meadow, stream, and forest. Tell the players they have one minute to find their special "listening place." Setting a definite time limit prevents restless players from walking around too long and disturbing the rest of the group. For the same reason, tell players to remain in their spots until you signal that the activity is over.

How long should you play? From 4 to 10 minutes is good—depending on the group's age and interest level, and on how active the animals are. Once you've called the group back together ask them to divide into pairs, each to share his sound map with a partner.

After players have shared their maps, you can ask them questions such as these:

- What sounds were the most familiar to you?
- What sound had you never heard before? Do you know what made the sound?
- What sound did you like best? Why?

Sitting quietly—listening to the soothing voices of nearby trees, birds, and rustling grasses—calms us and deepens our appreciation for the life around us. *Sound Map* is an excellent activity for instilling greater awareness of one's surroundings.

"This earth was the most glorious musical instrument, and I was audience to its strains."

—Thoreau

CAMOUFLAGE TRAIL

Camouflage Trail is one of my favorite games because both children and adults become concentrated and purposeful while trying to spot hard-to-see, hidden objects.

The leader places 16 to 24 manufactured objects along a section of trail 50 to 75 feet long. The objects should blend in with the vegetation and ground cover. Each player tries to see as many of the camouflaged objects as he can. "This game," I tell the players, "is an individual, not a team sport."

Setting forth on a *Camouflage Trail*, players immediately become sharp-eyed and focused as they search for such objects as a rusty nail, a brown penny, and a wooden clothespin. The game increases players' observational skills. After finishing the *Camouflage Trail*, one ten-year-old boy told me, "I saw a lizard blink from thirteen feet away."

To play, first assemble a collection of objects, some easy to see (such as a large, plastic fluorescent insect) and some more challenging. If you're playing with young children, the objects should be larger and easier to spot.

Choose a 50- to 75-foot section of trail or a clear area that has a variety of trees, plants, and leaf litter. (It's helpful if the path is wide enough for at least two people to pass by each other.) To help keep the players on the path and away from the hidden objects, mark the length of the *Camouflage Trail* with a piece of rope. The area should be relatively free of low-growing plants so that players can see the ground. For variety,

VISUAL AWARENESS, CONCENTRATION
• Day / forest, thicket
• For 1 to 30 people
• Ages 5 and up
• Manufactured objects, 75-foot length of rope

place objects at different heights and distances from the rope, but none farther than four feet horizontally from the rope.

Tell the players, "Walk carefully and count the total number of objects you see. You do not have to remember the different objects." To add suspense, keep the total number of hidden items a secret. As players finish the trail, they whisper to you the number of objects they have seen. In response, you might say, "Good, you've spotted one third of the total number." Or "Excellent, you've found three out of every four objects."

Because players will be eager to find *all* the items, invite them to walk the trail again. After everyone has finished, gather the group at the beginning of the trail. Ask the players to walk with you along the trail, and to call out when you approach one of the hidden objects. The leader can ask a volunteer to keep a running count (out loud) of the objects collected as he returns each one to the bag.

You can keep older children and adults engaged longer by including one or two cleverly camouflaged objects. My favorite is a 3" x 4" metal camping mirror, which can be aimed downward to reflect the forest litter. Covering the mirror's edge with a small branch makes it nearly impossible to find.

If the group is large, to allow everyone to play at the same time, you can have half the players walk the whole trail from beginning to end, and have the other half start midway on the trail, walk to the end, then double back to the beginning and walk to the midpoint.

You can, if you wish, end the game by discussing concepts such as adaptation and camouflage, and look for animals that demonstrate protective coloration.

ANIMALS, ANIMALS!

Sarah curled up in front of us and yawned. As our group of forty watched, she carefully lifted her left hand to her mouth, licked the back of her hand and gently rubbed it against her cheek. Instantly, we knew she was a cat. She then crouched low, her entire body tensed and alert. She sprang forward and pounced on an invisible prey. Mountain Lion! we called out, amid laughter and applause.

Animals, Animals! helps people develop a stronger affinity with animals. There are two ways to play the game. The first version, using animal pictures, is heartwarming and fun; while the second is more serious, often profound, and creates greater empathy through observing live animals.

WILDLIFE OBSERVATION, ANIMAL MOVEMENT, BEHAVIOR, EMPATHY
• Day and night / anywhere
• For 6 or more people
• Ages 5 and up
• Pictures of animals

FIRST VERSION
For groups of ten or fewer players:

Place the animal pictures face down; have participants pick a picture but keep their animal's identity secret. Ask the players to go off and practice acting out their animal's behavior and movement for a few minutes. Then call everyone together and have players, one at a time, act out their animals.

For large groups:

Ask for 6 to 8 volunteers to role-play their animals for the group. Place a variety of animal picture cards face up on the ground, and let each player choose the animal he feels best able to imitate.

Tell performers each to visualize his animal and capture its essence in a still pose, and to hold the pose for about six seconds. Afterwards, each can begin to move and behave like the animal chosen, but  without making any sounds. Ask the audience to watch in silence.

Let each actor finish his performance before you give the audience a chance to guess what the animal is. To keep the audience from guessing early, tell them you'll wave an arm when it's okay to begin guessing. If the audience cannot guess the animal, you can give them a subtle clue. But you'll be surprised by the marvelous imitations most players create. Almost always someone guesses the animal quickly.

Designating an area as the "stage" adds to the fun. So that you can help the audience with a clue if necessary, ask to see each player's animal card before the performance begins.

The animals you choose should be well-known, with easily identifiable physical characteristics, movements, and behavior. Some perennial favorites are bear, bat, penguin, gorilla, turtle, owl, leopard, and heron.

SECOND VERSION

While visiting a zoo, farm, or wild area, you can promote keen observation of animals by telling your group that you'll be asking them to choose an animal to act out for the rest of the group. If the players are mature enough, have each one go alone to look for an animal he finds interesting. Remind the players that dragonflies, lizards, and butterflies are animals, too. Tell each player to observe the chosen animals closely—then to imagine being that animal, and finally, to practice its movements and behavior.

MICRO-HIKE

Recently a woman told me that she has never forgotten the *Micro-Hike* she went on twenty-five years ago. "I had no idea," she said, "how many amazing things live on a tiny patch of soil."

Children are fascinated by the tiny world that lies just beneath them. In this game players go on a very small "hike." Give each child a piece of string that is 3 to 5 feet long, and ask them to find an intriguing patch of ground where they will lay out their string to mark the trail for their *Micro-Hike*.

Give each child a magnifying glass of 3x* power and show them how to use it to look at the minuscule rocks, plants, and bugs beneath them. Their heads must be about one foot above the ground for the best view. As they crawl on their belly or hands and knees, they might see little insects, tiny seeds, lichens, or flowers.

Ask if they can see signs that animals have chewed a leaf or eaten a seed. Encourage the children to feel that they're entering a magical, miniature world full of new sights and adventures. If they see a fascinating insect, ask them to learn as much as they can about it by observing it.

OBSERVATION OF
SOIL SURFACE
• Day / anywhere
• 1 person or more
• Ages 4 and up
• 3' to 5' length of string, 1 magnifying glass per player

Children do not have to finish the entire length of the trail. Sometimes a single foot will keep them engrossed for many minutes. Play this game for ten or fifteen minutes, then call all the participants together to share their discoveries.

* For an even closer look try a 5x power magnifying glass.

DUPLICATION

This game introduces
children to their natural sur-
roundings and awakens their interest in plants, rocks, and animals. The
leader displays eight natural objects and asks the players to memorize
them. The children are then to find duplicates of the displayed objects.

Before playing, walk around the immediate area and gather eight
objects, such as a pinecone, a rock, a dried seedpod, an acorn, a fallen
tree leaf—and something from an animal, such as a feather, a tuft of
fur on a bush, or the abandoned exoskeleton of a dragonfly nymph.
(Whatever you collect must be common enough in the area for each
child to find similar objects. Do not use anything that's alive, such as
a flower or an insect.) Lay the objects on one bandana and cover them
with the other bandana.

Gather the children around you and explain
that you'll display some natural objects that can
be found nearby. Tell them, "You have 25 seconds
to look at the objects and remember them. Then
each of you will go and collect similar items."
Pull back the top bandana and display the items
for the time allotted, then replace the bandana.

MEMORY, VISUAL
AWARENESS,
NATURAL HISTORY
- Day / anywhere
- For 2 or more people
- Ages 5 and up
- 2 bandanas

When the children return with their items, gather everyone around
the original objects. Place your hand under the top bandana, grasp
one of the objects, and tell an informative story about it. For example,
"Native Americans used this item for food, bait for animal traps, and
to make tops and other toys." Then, dramatically, bring out the acorn
and show it to the children, and ask, "Who found an acorn from the
black oak tree?" Because the children have been looking for an acorn,
as well as for other objects, they've built up an interest in knowing
more about each one.

SLEEPING MISER

Here's a challenge children can't resist: to sneak up on a sleeping miser and steal his bag of gold. Children must approach so quietly that the miser never hears them. This stalking game fosters self-control and deep attention, and encourages being quiet outdoors.

Ask one child to play the miser: he sits on the ground blindfolded and with a hat or scarf in front of him to represent his bag of gold. Though deeply possessive of his treasure, the miser has now fallen asleep. The other children use this opportunity to try to grab his treasure.

Choose an area where the stalkers will make a little, but not a lot of noise. The stalkers form a ring around the miser (about 20 feet away), and can walk barefooted if they wish. At your signal, with the goal of grabbing the treasure, stalkers begin to walk as quietly as possible toward the miser. To succeed, the children must be in control of each movement of their bodies; no running or diving for the treasure is allowed.

STALKING,
CONCENTRATION

• Day / clearing
• For 5 or more people
• Ages 6 and up
• Blindfold

The "referee" stands behind the miser. If the miser hears a sound, he points in the direction of that sound. The referee "seconds" the point if the sound was loud enough. The referee may allow some of the miser's points to go un-seconded; but if he does point to a child, that child must stop and hold his position for the time being.

After several players have been "caught," or have touched the treasure, the referee calls a time out. During the break, players who've touched the treasure move to the edge of the circle and wait for the other players to finish. Those who have been caught go back to the edge of the circle and start over. Make sure that no one advances toward the treasure during time outs. The first player to touch the treasure is the miser for the next round.

Because children are quiet during this game, seldom-seen animals often enter the area, to everyone's delight. But the key benefits of *Sleeping Miser* are the skills players learn: self-control and alert attention.

WATCHER OF THE ROAD

In this night game, one player sits in the middle of an untraveled road as the Watcher. His eyes are closed and he holds a flashlight. The other players try to sneak past him without being heard.

Have the players form a line across the road, fifteen feet from the Watcher. Several children at a time walk as quietly as they can, trying to reach home base, located ten feet past the Watcher. If the Watcher hears a sound, he aims the flashlight at the source of the sound. (It's not fair to sweep the flashlight around in hopes of hitting someone with the beam!) Any child touched by the flashlight beam must stop moving.

After several players have been caught, call a time out to allow those players to return to the starting line and begin again. The first child to reach home base safely becomes the next Watcher.

CONCENTRATION, STALKING
- Night / road
- For 5 or more people
- Ages 5 to 13
- Flashlight

OFFER DIRECT EXPERIENCE
Activities

During magical encounters with nature, we are like a cell fed by osmosis—we are absorbing our immediate environment. The direct experience activities in this section fully immerse us in the natural world.

once read that indigenous tribes wade in marshes at night to hunt ducks. The blackness of night enables them to approach the birds closely.

As a birder, I was intrigued by the possibilities. One winter evening, I visited my favorite marsh to see if this account was true. As I approached the marsh, I heard thousands of geese tremble, then take off with a thunderous roar, wings slapping hard for momentum. The flock erupted like a volcano, filling the sky with swirling, milling geese.

Skimming over the wetland grasses were thousands of ducks flying in every direction. Oblivious to the wintry cold, I hurried into the water. The vibrancy of the marsh with its fast-flying ducks and V-shaped strings of clamoring geese awoke in me a euphoria so great that I easily ignored any discomfort.

The moonless night hid my presence, and flocks of ducks began flying unusually close. Whistles, whirs, peeps, and quacks filled

my ears—exhilarating!—ducks were landing all around me like big falling raindrops.

Sensing something above me, I looked up and saw a great horned owl swoop by. Since only my head was above water, the curious owl had flown in for a closer look. Meanwhile, ducks were swimming all around me, some coming so close I could almost touch them. Later, as I was standing completely still in shallow water, a small duck swam calmly between my legs.

For hours I waded silently from one duck-filled pond to another, using my ears and hands to guide me. The experience of the marsh at night—teeming with ducks and geese—was so engrossing that boundaries of separation seemed to blur, or even disappear.

INTERVIEW WITH NATURE

In this activity, you choose a rock, a plant, an animal, or a natural feature that has an interesting story to tell. For example, you can pick a dragonfly, a yellow flower, a boulder, a mountain peak, or even the wind.

Get to know your choice as well as you can. Try to learn about it in as many different ways as possible. For example, if you choose a rock or plant, you can feel its texture with your hands. See if anything grows on it. Look for evidence that something—such as fire, drought, or erosion—might have harmed or affected it in some way. Stand a short distance away and see how it fits into and interacts with its surroundings.

Imagine what its life might be like, and tell what you admire about it. Think also about the kinds of life experiences it might have had. Geologists have said that some rocks in the Grand Canyon are two billion years old. It's fun to think of all the things that have happened to those rocks since their creation. Mountain ranges have risen and fallen, deserts have come and gone, and seas have arrived and departed. Dinosaurs, mammoths, and camels have all in their turns walked the land.

While interviewing your subject and writing answers to your questions, try to see life from its point of view. Because your rock, plant, or animal cannot talk to you in the human sense, use your imagination to come up with the answers; if you like, you can try listening quietly for thoughts that tell you how your friend might respond.

EVERYTHING IS ALIVE, EMPATHY
- Day / anywhere
- For 2 or more people
- Ages 7 and up
- Pencils, paper, interview questions

Wild animals and plants attract us because we have a natural affinity for those sharing the gift of life. Humanizing nature helps us feel to some degree that all beings are like us.

HOW TO PLAY: Select the category that matches your subject, then ask *and* answer the questions that most apply. Feel free to make up your own questions and conversations. Adults with young children can read the questions aloud and write down their children's answers.

ROCK, NATURAL FEATURE, or PLANT

- How old are you?
- Where did you come from?
- Have you always been the size you are now?
- What is it like living in this particular place?
- What events have you seen in your life?
- Who comes to visit you?
- How do you benefit others?
- How do they help you?
- Is there something special you would like to tell me?

ANIMAL Look for an animal that's easy to observe. It might be an insect, lizard, or ground squirrel. Imagine yourself becoming the animal. Try not to disturb or frighten it. Ask *and* answer some of the questions below:

- What are you doing now?
- Where do you live?
- What do you eat, and how do you find your food?
- How does your life benefit others?
- How do they help you?
- What are the things you like most about your life?
- Do you ever travel to other places?
- What would you like to tell others about yourself?

Give the players about ten minutes for their interviews, and then call them back. As they return, ask them to gather in teams of three or four and share their interviews with one another.

OBSERVE NATURE
LIKE JOHN MUIR

"I'd sit for hours watching
the birds or squirrels, or looking into
the faces of flowers. When I discovered a new
plant, I sat beside it for a minute or a day, to
make its acquaintance and try to hear what it had to tell me."

*—John Muir: My Life with Nature**

Most people *look* but don't *see*. This activity helps you discover and remember the physical characteristics and special quality of an animal.

Choose an animal that is easy to observe, such as a bird, frog, or insect. To see your animal well, use binoculars or a magnifying glass if you have them. If you can't find an animal to observe, choose a tree, flower, or even a rock or river.

CREATIVE WRITING,
OBSERVATION,
EMPATHY

• Day / anywhere
• For 1 person or more
• Ages 10 and up
• Pencils, paper

As you study your special animal (or plant, etc.), look for characteristics you've never noticed before—the color of its eyes, how it moves, or the texture or pattern of its leaves or feathers.

A) List seven things you've discovered about your animal or plant.

1. _____
2. _____
3. _____
4. _____
5. _____
6. _____
7. _____

* John Muir paraphrased by Joseph Cornell, *John Muir: My Life with Nature* (Nevada City, CA: Dawn Publications, 2000), 28.

B) Choose a word that describes how your animal moves (or stands, if it is a plant):

_____

C) Write a word or phrase that expresses the unique spirit of your animal or plant:

_____

D) If you were to give your animal or plant a name, what would it be, and why?

_____

E) Write a simple poem or story about your animal or plant. Tell what you admire about it.
Before you start, read John Muir's account of western junipers. Muir saw everything as alive with its own unique beauty.

WESTERN JUNIPER
by John Muir*

The Sierra juniper is one of the hardiest of all mountaineers. Growing mostly on ridges and rocks, these brave highlanders live for over twenty centuries on sunshine and snow. Thick and sturdy, junipers easily survive mountain storms. A truly wonderful fellow, he seems to last about as long as the granite he stands on. Surely he is the most enduring of all tree mountaineers—never seeming to die a natural death. If protected from accidents, he would perhaps be immortal. I wish I could live like these junipers, on sunshine and snow, and stand beside them for a thousand years. How much I should see, and how delightful it would be!

---

* John Muir paraphrased by Joseph Cornell, *John Muir: My Life with Nature* (Nevada City, CA: Dawn Publications, 2000), 65.

CAMERA

Because *Camera* quiets distracting thoughts and restlessness so that one can see clearly, this exercise is one of the most powerful and memorable in the book.

Camera is played with two people: one person is the photographer and the other the camera. The photographer guides the camera, who has his eyes closed, on a search for beautiful and captivating pictures. When the photographer sees something he likes, he points the camera at it, to frame the object he wants to shoot.

The photographer signals the camera to open the lens (his eyes) by tapping twice on the camera's shoulder. A third tap 3 seconds later tells the camera to close his eyes again. For the first picture, it may help to say "Open" with the first two taps, and "Close" with the third.

AESTHETIC APPRECIATION
• Day / outdoor area
• For 2 or more people
• Ages 4 and up, with adult / Ages 12 and up
• Index cards, pencils

Have the camera keep his eyes closed between pictures—to give the three-second "exposure" the impact of surprise. Encourage photographer and camera to walk in silence (speaking only if absolutely necessary) to enhance the camera's experience.

Participants have often told me that they've remembered the images of their photographs for more than five years. In addition to the visual power of the exercise, the camera, during his peri-

ods of sightlessness, will also experience a magnification of his other senses.

After taking 4 to 6 photographs, the camera and the photographer trade roles.

Because the experience is so compelling, a beautiful rapport is established between the photographer and the human camera. It's heartwarming to observe grandparents and grandchildren, and other pairings, carefully guide each other and delight in the wondrous scenes of nature around them.

You can experience by yourself how *Camera* intensifies awareness. Select an area of varied terrain that's mostly clear of obstructions. Since you'll be walking alone, take along a hiking staff or pole for security and guidance.

Choose a safe route leading to interesting features such as large rocks, trees, or an arresting view. Close your eyes and begin walking. Notice how your leg muscles compensate for the unevenness of the terrain. Feel the warmth of the sun and the wind blowing against your body, and listen to the insects singing and buzzing close by.

As you walk, you can (as needed to stay on course) open your eyes just enough to detect blurry shapes.

When you sense that you're near something intriguing, open your eyes to take its picture. Opening your eyes for only the suggested three seconds keeps the attention sharply focused on the subject the whole time. When the exposures are longer, the mind tends to wander.

Continue to tread carefully while taking a few more photographs.

More CAMERA tips:

1. Sensitively guide the camera by holding his hand and gently pulling his arm in the direction you want to go. Go slowly and remain watchful for obstacles on the ground and for low-lying tree branches.

2. Make the photographs stunning by taking shots from unusual angles and perspectives. For example, you can both lie down under a tree and take your picture looking upward, or you can put your camera very close to a tree's bark or leaves.

3. You can prepare the camera's vision for the next picture by telling him which lens to use. For a picture of a flower, tell the camera to choose a close-up lens; for a sweeping scenic panorama, a wide-angle lens; and for a far-away object, a telephoto lens.

4. Photographers can also pan the camera, i.e., move it slowly with the shutter held open, like a movie camera. While panning, you can keep the shutter open longer, since the movement will hold the camera's interest. You can also pan vertically—for example, start at the base of a tree and slowly move up the trunk to the highest branches.

5. After participants have played both roles, each player can "develop" (sketch from memory) one of the pictures he took while he was the camera. Then have each camera give his developed picture to his photographer.

Guidelines for playing
CAMERA *with children:*

Children younger than twelve years normally should pair with an adult or mature teenager. Younger children don't have enough awareness of others to allow them to guide another child. It is, however, fine to have a young child lead a parent or grandparent. In this situation, I recommend letting the adult camera know it's okay to peek from time to time.

If children will be leading each other, it's helpful to have them first sit blindfolded in a small circle and pass around fascinating natural objects. Activities such as *Caterpillar Walk* and *Blind Rope Walk* help children become more at ease while walking blindfolded. Once children are comfortable moving with their eyes closed, they'll be ready and keen to play the *Camera* game.

To ensure safety, you can have the camera stand behind the photographer with his hands on the photographer's shoulders. As the photographer begins to walk, the camera will follow directly behind, and thus will avoid low-lying tree limbs and other obstacles. Using this method, adult leaders can guide three or four child cameras at a time.

Make sure to tell players about any potential dangers such as poisonous plants, harmful insect nests, or animal holes.

"See how willingly Nature poses herself upon photographers' plates. No earthly chemicals are so sensitive as those of the human soul."

—John Muir

BIRD CALLING

Birds symbolize freedom
and elegance, and they're some of
our planet's most endearing animals. The best way to interest people
in birds is to give them close, intimate bird encounters. Fortunately,
there is an easy-to-make call that attracts small birds close to you. It's
magical to see them just yards away, flitting from branch to branch.
Many friends and students of mine have become lifelong bird enthu-
siasts after using this call and witnessing its effectiveness. This call,
however, should be used judiciously—be especially careful not to use
it if it might disturb rare or nesting birds.

The bird call consists of a simple "pssh" sound repeated in a slow,
regular tempo, three to five times:

pssh . . . pssh . . . pssh . . . pssh

Practice three to five sets of the call, pause, watch and listen for
incoming birds, then repeat.

Birders call this practice "pishing"; they also use other syllables,
such as pssst, sip, and seep. Experiment to see what syllables and tempo
work best on the birds in your region. Because birds will either respond
quickly or not respond at all, if they don't react
immediately, it's not productive to keep calling.

When you hear or see birds in the vicin-
ity, sit or stand near the branches of a tree or
shrub before beginning to call. (This position
allows the birds to land close to you.) As the
birds approach, repeat the "pssh" sound now
and again to keep them close.

ATTRACTING BIRDS
• Day and night /
thicket, forest
• For 1 person or more
• Ages 5 and up
• Binoculars optional

Many times, fifty or more birds have responded to the call, some coming within a few feet of me. Once a mountain chickadee flew out of its nesting hole in a nearby tree and landed on my shoulder.

There are several theories as to why pishing attracts birds. One theory is that the "pssh" sound matches in tonal quality the sounds small birds make when they surround and harass predators to drive them out of their area. This anti-predator behavior is called "mobbing."

Once in the Sierra Mountains, seven Boy Scouts and I witnessed a dramatic occurrence of mobbing. As we sat in a thicket of low-growing alder trees, a pine marten (a small weasel that eats birds) scampered to within eight feet, stopped and gazed intently at us. To keep the marten curious, I made the "pssh" distress call. In less than a minute, ten birds flew in like the U.S. Cavalry—warblers, vireos, chickadees, and kinglets—and immediately made scolding noises at the intruder.

While using the "pssh" call, you can play a recording of a screech owl call. (The diet of this small owl includes insects, small mammals, and birds.) I've had as many as seventy-five birds respond to the interplay of the two calls. First play the screech owl recording, pause, then make the "pssh" call for twenty seconds or so; you can continue alternating the calls. Combining "pssh" and owl calls simulates birds scolding a living owl.

The *Sharing Nature Audio Resources* CD includes a recording of a calling screech owl. This recording also is available with *Sharing Nature Online Resources* at *www.sharenature.org*.

Because the screech owl call is so effective you should not use it during the breeding season.

MYSTERY ANIMAL

Years ago, I was wandering in the fields near my home when I saw a beautiful bird, about the size of a robin, but smaller and thinner. I had never seen such a striking bird. Its head and back were black, its eyes were red, its sides were chestnut-colored, and its belly was white. Its back and wings were covered with dazzling white spots. When it flew, there was a flashing display of browns, whites, and blacks. I didn't know anyone who could tell me the bird's name, nor did I have the trained eye of a birder to enable me to find its picture amidst the hundreds of others in a bird field guide.

Every day for two weeks, I went out to look at these birds. I discovered that they fed on the ground by pulling up leaves and twigs to uncover seeds and insects. They scratched in the leaves so vigorously that they sometimes made more noise than a deer. They gave a trilling call and also a cat-like "meow." To me, these birds were marvelous and mysterious.

My interest in these birds grew into a lifelong love for birding. Not finding a quick answer to my questions taught me that the longer curiosity burns, the more we learn. All profound knowing is born of mystery and revelation.

By the way, the bird was a spotted towhee.

NATURAL HISTORY.
DRAWING

- Day and night / anywhere
- For 3 or more people
- Ages 5 and up
- Picture of Mystery Animal, pencils, index cards

Mystery Animal Overview

In *Mystery Animal*, you have the players close their eyes and listen carefully as you lead them on an imaginary journey. When you have brought them to their destination, they will observe and learn about a particular animal, without ever knowing its name. After returning from the journey, they try to draw the animal. Amid great laughter, players show their wildly different drawings to one another. Then, you show them a photograph of the animal.

The players' attempt to accurately draw the *Mystery Animal* ignites their curiosity; they're keen to see the animal's true likeness. When participants finally view the animal's photograph, they gaze in wonder at every nuance of the animal's form.

Mystery Animal gives players the opportunity to view an animal's form with fresh eyes, untainted by preconception. Because of the intensity of attention in this activity, players retain a strong impression of the animal.

Read the *Mystery Animal* narrative below. After you finish reading, try to draw a picture of the animal.

A Mystery Animal

You are in one of the last unexplored places on earth. Charles Darwin called this region "one great, wild, luxuriant hothouse." The temperature is usually over eighty degrees Fahrenheit, the humidity eighty percent, and the average annual rainfall thirteen feet. Because of its favorable growing conditions, the tropical rainforest harbors a greater variety of life than any other environment.

Look up at the trees above you. Because the dense forest canopy allows only five percent of the sun's light to reach the ground, the forest floor is relatively free of ground cover. As you stroll through the forest, you see many new and fascinating plants, and hear a chorus of wild, shrieking, croaking, and clicking cries. You ask yourself, "Who are the owners of these strange voices—monkeys, birds, frogs, or insects?"

Looking up, you see something move high on a branch. It looks like a mass of dead leaves, moldy fungus, or perhaps a termite's nest. But, wait—it moved again! Use your binoculars to get a closer look. It's an animal—with long, coarse hair and four long limbs. The animal is about two feet long and seems to weigh around fourteen pounds. Its rounded head is no bigger than its neck, and it doesn't have any ears that you can see. It's very hard to tell which end is the front and which is the rear, because you can't see a tail. Aha! Its face is turning toward you. Study it closely. Its face is flat and whitish, and its mouth wears a perpetual smile.

This animal isn't known for its speed; in fact, it moves like a slow-motion movie. It's beginning to move now, ever so slowly—one limb at a time. See it reach slowly for the branch nearest to it. It's almost got it. (Pause) There! Now watch its other leg begin to move. It may take half a minute to shift its legs only a few inches.

One mother, hurrying to her baby fifteen feet away, covered the distance in just over an hour. This animal's slow movement is its greatest protection, because its sluggishness makes it difficult for its main enemies, jaguars and harpy eagles, to detect. Its top speed in the trees is a little over one mile per hour, but on land it moves at only one-tenth of a mile per hour: because its legs can't support its weight, it has to drag itself along the ground. It doesn't come down from the trees very often—only to give birth and to defecate. Defecation occurs infrequently—once every seven or eight days.

One scientist jokingly remarked that some people would think this animal has an ideal life. After observing the animal for one week, he gave this report of how it spent its time:

11 hours feeding   **10** hours resting
18 hours just moving slowly about   **129** hours sleeping

It spends 18 out of every 24 hours sleeping.* Its metabolism is so slow that it can survive under water for as long as thirty minutes.

---

* Recent studies have shown, however, that this animal sleeps less than scientists previously thought.

This animal doesn't spend a lot of time on personal hygiene. Living in the fur of one individual were found 978 beetles, divided among four species; also living happily in its hair were nine species of moths, six species of ticks, and several species of mites.

During the rainy season, the algae growing in its fur flourishes, and the resultant greenish tint serves as camouflage. Caterpillars feed on its moldy hair, pupate, and continue to live as adults in its fur.

This forest dweller is so primitive and slow-witted you wonder how it survives. Its success is due to its inertia, its protective coloration, its habit of feeding mostly at night, and its twenty-three pairs of ribs, thick fur and tough skin, all of which protect its internal organs.

Our animal is doing what it does best: sleeping. Let's take one last look at it hanging upside down from a branch. Notice its four long limbs, each with three long, curved claws; no apparent neck, tail, or ears; globular head, and whitish, smiling face; and coarse hair hanging down toward its spine.

Now that you've returned home, open your eyes, and draw a picture of the animal. Then compare your drawing with the picture of the *Mystery Animal* on page 195.

HOW TO PLAY and create your own Mystery Animal:

1. Choose an animal that has fascinating behavior and striking physical features. If you pick a familiar animal, make it seem exotic by sharing little-known information, as in the following example:

- Each offspring has thousands of brothers and sisters.

- It can see forwards, sideways, partially behind, and upward at the same time.

- It breathes fifty per cent of its air through its skin and drinks its water entirely through its skin. *The animal is a frog.*

2. Use sensory words to paint a vivid picture of its environment. For example, if the animal lives in the tropical rainforest, you could mention the lushness and dankness of the forest.

3. To keep listeners engaged, create a lively, concise narrative.

4. Ideally, memorize a few key parts of the script and narrate the rest of the visualization extemporaneously.

5. If players are self-conscious about their ability to draw, tell them they can sign another person's name on their drawing to give someone else the credit!

6. After players have drawn their pictures, tell them, "It's time now for our scientific symposium. I want each scientist to share his Field Report (drawing of the *Mystery Animal*) with at least four other scientists." As the players scrutinize one another's drawings, there's a lot of laugher.

7. Ask the players if they'd like to see a photograph of the animal, then show the *Mystery Animal* picture. The players' enthusiasm will amaze you. Faces glow with concentration as they search the photograph for details you've mentioned and that they've included in their drawings.

For Children:

Instead of having children ages five and six draw the *Mystery Animal*, you can show pictures of five different animals and ask the children to choose the correct animal.

This is a great activity for a zoo field trip. Before taking the children to see the animals, share the *Mystery Animal* narrative and ask them to see if they can spot the animal in the zoo. It's touching to watch young children look intently at each animal, trying to determine whether it's the *Mystery Animal*. To keep the children engaged, you can arrange for the *Mystery Animal* to come toward the end of your route.

Appendix C:

The *Mystery Animal* is a three-toed sloth. It lives in the tropical rainforests of Central and South America.

MEET A TREE

Trees, said Buddha, have unlimited kindness and benevolence, and uplift the human spirit. Scientific studies show that trees calm us and provide spiritual and creative inspiration.

Meet a Tree connects us with trees in a memorable way. To play, divide the group into pairs and have one of each pair wear a blindfold. The seeing player—if old enough—leads the blindfolded player to a special tree, one that has intriguing characteristics. Upon meeting the tree, the blindfolded player feels the texture of the tree's bark, sees how big the tree is by putting his arms around it, and explores the tree's branches and leaves. The guide can silently guide the player's hands to interesting places on and around the tree.

One Sharing Nature leader in Japan often tells children, "In this forest there is a tree that has been waiting to meet you since before you were born." The children, touched by these words, are honored and eager to meet their tree.

After getting to know their trees, the blindfolded players are brought back to the starting point, where their blindfolds are removed. They then try to find their tree. Most adults and children (except for the very young) who have walked blindfolded

FOREST APPRECIATION, SENSORY AWARENESS, EMPATHY

- Day / forest
- For 2 or more people
- Ages 4 and up
- Blindfolds

thirty yards or more to a tree, can find it later with open eyes. Leaders should, however, adapt the distance to the age, mobility, and the ability of the players to orient themselves in nature.

Faces of both children and adult players immediately glow with elation when they recognize their tree—it is as though two dear friends have reunited.

Children younger than twelve should probably be paired with an adult. Young children may also want to guide their adult friends: if so, the adult can look as needed for safety purposes.

CATERPILLAR WALK

Blindfold activities promote alertness by awakening the senses. You can use *Caterpillar Walk* to help your group travel attentively through magical areas such as a sunlit forest clearing alive with calling birds, or as a way to heighten awareness for a spectacular view. For example, I once used *Caterpillar Walk* to prepare a group for their first view of the Grand Canyon.

SENSORY AWARENESS, WONDER

- **Day / anywhere**
- **For 2 to 4 people**
- **Ages 10 and up**
- **Blindfolds**

Arrange children in a line of two to four players. (Having more than four "segments" of the caterpillar can be too unwieldy.) Blindfold the caterpillar segments and have each child place his hands on the shoulders of the child in front.

Have an adult leader or mature adolescent lead each caterpillar. Leaders should encourage the blindfolded caterpillar players to become aware of their surroundings by using their ears and hands. Stop frequently to let them feel unusual trees, rocks, or to smell scented bushes. Because a varied trail is the most captivating, plan your route to take in objects of special interest such as, for example, wind flowing upward through a lush canyon or a spongy bog.

Once you've come to the end of your walk, remove the blindfolds and have the children gaze at the spectacular view. Before starting back, I sometimes have the children draw a sensory map of the trail they've traversed. This map could include a variety of sensory experiences—

smells, sounds, the feeling of walking through a moist meadow or a field of massive boulders. Then I let the group find their way home by using the sensory clues as signposts.

JOURNEY TO THE HEART OF NATURE

Helen, a participant in one of my Sharing Nature workshops, told me a delightful story from her birding trip to Kenya. While she was standing with a couple of friends at a trail crossing, five Masai tribesmen walked up. Helen wanted to ask them if a certain bird lived nearby, but couldn't speak their language.

She flipped through her bird book and showed the Masai a picture of the bird she wanted to see. The Masai men smiled, began to imitate the bird's behavior, then pointed to where it could be found. The birders, thrilled to have such knowledgeable guides, showed the Masai several more pictures. The Masai mimicked each bird's mannerisms and pointed to its likely whereabouts. Helen was amazed at how well the Masai knew the local birds.

Then, without being shown a picture, the Masai acted out a bird of their own choosing. Now it was the birders' turn to demonstrate their knowledge of African birds. Helen looked through the book until she found the bird she thought the Masai were mimicking. Five delighted smiles told Helen her guess was right.

Native people's intimate knowledge of their environment comes from living close to nature. *Journey to the Heart of Nature* gives us the opportunity to immerse ourselves in a particular natural spot—to listen to the land and enter fully into the lives of its inhabitants.

The exercises below, from the Explorer's Guide for *Journey to the Heart of Nature*, focus and enhance our experience of a natural place.

EXPLORATION
AWARENESS OF
NATURE,
REFLECTION

- Day / natural area
- For 2 or more people
- Ages 10 and up
- Explorer's Guide
  per player, pencils,
  clipboards,
  invitation cards

In this activity, each explorer finds a place outdoors that he especially enjoys. During his visit there (about 25 minutes), he chooses a name for his special place and writes it on a card. Later, he will use the card to invite a friend to his area, and he'll also visit his friend's site.

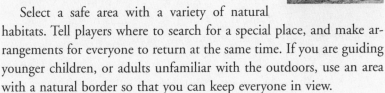

You Are Invited to Explore:

THE GIANT FOREST

Your Guide Is:

JOSEPH

Knowing that they'll later be entertaining a guest and sharing their discoveries, explorers give the *Journey to the Heart of Nature* experience their full attention. Sharing their special place is a highlight for the explorers, and a marvelous way for people to connect with one another.

Select a safe area with a variety of natural habitats. Tell players where to search for a special place, and make arrangements for everyone to return at the same time. If you are guiding younger children, or adults unfamiliar with the outdoors, use an area with a natural border so that you can keep everyone in view.

Pass out Explorer Guides, pencils, writing boards, and invitation cards. Briefly explain the activities in the Guides and then ask each person to find his own area. When the allotted time has passed, call everyone back.

To share places:

Have half the players put their invitation cards into your hat; then have each of those who still have a card pick another card out of the hat, then pair up with the owner of the new card. Let's say that Sally draws George's card: Sally keeps his card and gives George her card. By exchanging cards, Sally and George have invited each other to their special places. Give pairs fifteen to twenty minutes to share both their places and the exercises they have practiced with one another.

Then assemble the group and go over the exercises one by one; allow participants to share with the rest of the group their place names, drawings, Vertical Poems, and whatever has inspired them.

EXPLORER'S GUIDE

Since you won't have time to do every exercise, choose the ones that are most interesting to you and that give you the greatest sense of involvement with your special place.

First Impressions | After choosing a Special Place, take the time to wander around to see what's there. Then pick a spot where you can think about your site, make yourself comfortable, and answer these questions:

1. What are the first things I notice about my site?
2. What do I like about being here?

What Do You Hear? | Listen to the symphony of sounds around you. Concentrate on the distant sounds, and then gradually shift your attention to nearby sounds.

Can you hear the trees singing with the wind? See if you can pick out the song one tree is singing and describe it.

Can you identify five different sounds and describe who or what is making them?

1. _____
2. _____
3. _____
4. _____
5. _____

Invitation Card | Choose a name for this special place.

The name of my site is: _____

Fill out the card with your name and the name of your site.

Sketch Your Best View
Find your favorite view and then draw it. You'll show your drawing to your guest, who will then try to find the view.

Share something that makes you smile inside.

Write a Vertical Poem
(*See the next page for this popular exercise.*)

Resources | If you would like access to the Explorer's Guide master handout in order to make duplicates, go to *Sharing Nature Online Resources* at www.sharenature.org.

VERTICAL POEM

Vertical Poem is a popular Explorer's Guide selection in the *Journey to the Heart of Nature* activity (page 140). It also can be used alone as a group bonding activity.

To practice *Vertical Poem*, first observe something that captivates you—perhaps a field of flowers or a secluded sea cove. Notice its effect on you, and choose a word that captures your feeling. Then use each letter of the word to begin a line of your poem.

REFLECTION,
SELF-EXPRESSION
• Day or night /
  indoors or outdoors
• For 1 person or more
• Ages 11 and up
• Paper, pencil(s),
  clipboard(s)

The simple structure of a vertical poem makes it very easy to write. After successfully crafting their verses, people have exclaimed to me, "It's been forty years since I've written a poem!"

In Taiwan I once led eighty people down a steep, narrow track to a stunning gorge. The trail and chasm were so confining that I couldn't gather the group together. *Vertical Poem*

was the perfect exercise for the setting. In the depths of the gorge, eighty people, immersed in the chasm scenery, composed their vertical poems. After climbing out of the canyon, many participants read their poems to the group—each poem beautifully expressing our shared experience of the gorge.

Composing a vertical poem quiets a group and allows people to become more present and immersed in their surroundings.

The *Vertical Poem* below was written in a forest in Northern California:

Fragrances of oak and pine
Open up the heart and mind.
Remain still awhile and listen:
Everywhere is Nature's song—
Sometimes as silent as a leaf falling;
Time is suspended.

—Tom W.

Vertical Poem

Write the word you've chosen, one letter on each line. Then use each letter to begin a line of your poem.

_____   _____

_____   _____

_____   _____

_____   _____

_____   _____

_____   _____

_____   _____

SUNSET WATCH

The glorious colors of a sunset lead into the magic of dusk and nightfall. During this period, the quiet viewer can observe many fascinating changes and events. Though we have all experienced the transition from daylight to nighttime every day of our lives, it's engrossing to practice this watchful, self-guided activity.

Below is a list of sunset events to give to each participant. Bring your group to the viewing spot fifteen minutes before the actual time of sunset, and stay as long afterwards as you like.

What you see will depend on the area and time of year. The list below offers occurrences that happen almost everywhere. Mark each event in the order it happens. For example, if you first notice that the day birds are quiet, you would write "1" next to *day birds*. If you hear an owl or other night bird a little later, write "2" for *owl calling*, and so on. If an event is continually changing, such as the clouds turning color, you can note the changes by writing more than one number for the event—for example, "5" and "8" *clouds change color*. Don't worry about missing something or getting the order exactly. Just put a number by events as you observe them.

ASTRONOMY,
WILDLIFE, SERENITY

- **Sunset / stunning view**
- **For 1 person or more**
- **Ages 9 and up**
- **Handout(s), pencils, flashlight**

Because each location is unique, you'll probably see events not on the list. You might observe a flock of birds gathering in a tree, for example, or a mammal beginning its evening ramble, fish jumping for flying insects, or frogs singing. Write down under *other events* any occurrence not on the list.

Make sure to look in all directions, not only toward the western sky where the sun is setting, and bring a flashlight to find your way home in the dark.

Intriguing facts about stars and seeing at night:

- Do you know that your night vision is actually better than a bear's and almost as good as a cat's? In order to have full night vision, we need 45 minutes for our eyes to recover after being in artificial light. Consequently, we rarely experience the full power of our night vision.

- Billions and billions of stars are known to exist. If we observe the night sky on a clear, moonless night, we might see about two thousand of them.

- Light travels at 186,000 miles a second. Yet some stars are so far away that it takes hundreds, thousands, or even millions of years for their light to reach us. When you look at a star, you may be seeing light that began its long journey hundreds of years ago.

- When we look at the stars we're looking back in time—seeing the universe as it was long ago.

Sunset Watch

Location: _____ *Date:* _____

____ First planet or star.

____ Long shadows.

____ Bats fly.

____ Everything to the east is lit by glory light.

____ Things far to the west lose their day color.

____ Day birds are quiet.

____ Hills turn color. (*describe*) _____
_____

____ Sky is dark except to the west.

____ Owl or other night bird calling or flying.

____ Campfire or lights of car or building become visible.

____ Clouds change color. (*describe*) _____
_____

____ Sun falls below the horizon.

____ Where you are individual shadows blend together.

____ Night insects become active.

____ Night shadow completely covers hills to the east.

____ Sky turns a soft pink or violet color (after sundown).

____ Moon appears or brightens.

____ Clouds are no longer visible.

____ North Star and Little Dipper or Southern Cross appear.

____ Temperature cools.

____ Wind speed or direction changes.

____ First shooting star or meteor appears.

____ *Other events:* Record and number any other events you notice
  (*for example, a satellite, or a wolf or coyote howling*)._____
_____

BLINDFOLD
ACTIVITIES

*The warmth of the sun, the call
of a solitary bird, the scent of wildflowers
wafting in the air—all these can touch us deeply when we're receptive and alert. Through the
physical senses we perceive the world around us.*

Many years ago, a naturalist at an Ohio outdoor education center led a group of children on a special hike. I participated that day and still enjoy my memories of the outing.

We were going to one of the few pine forests in southern Ohio. Most of the children had never been in an evergreen forest before. The children were excited, and our naturalist-guide channeled their high energy skillfully to create a moving experience of the forest.

She first took us to a Christmas-tree farm, where she announced with a flourishing sweep of an arm and a twinkle in her eye, "Here is the pine forest." Groans and shuffling feet testified to the group's disappointment—the trees were barely taller than the children.

She then blindfolded each person and led us through a sunny de-ciduous forest, where we enjoyed the sounds of rustling leaves and chattering birds. Then, as we heard a stream splashing, the naturalist said, "There's a narrow bridge here, so you'll have to cross one at a time." The first child started bravely across, then shrieked with nervous laughter. The rest of us waited uneasily, not knowing what was ahead.

My turn came, and I groped my way forward, taking a first cau-tious step onto the bridge. Aha! No wonder there were squeals—the bridge swayed dizzily from side to side, and bounced up and down at the same time. Between the creaks and groans of ropes and wood, I heard water rushing far below me.

At the other side I was greeted by a flutter of small hands; the naturalist and her helpers had let the children take off their blindfolds to watch me cross. I removed my own blindfold and saw a strong suspension bridge, its handrails polished from much use.

We replaced our blindfolds and struck out on the trail again. Soon, the sound of our footsteps changed: instead of crackling leaves, we heard soft, muffled crunching sounds. Then, a dark shadow surrounded us, and we sensed a deep quiet. A child's voice broke the silence: "Where are we?"

The naturalist said, "Lie down on your backs and feel what is special about this place."

For a time we enjoyed the serene, restful quiet. Then, the naturalist told us to take off our blindfolds. Shooting skyward were countless towering pine trees. My spirits rose with the trees, and I was overwhelmed with admiration for the inspired wisdom in creating such a dramatic experience for each of us—I had never felt so moved by a forest. The children, too, were stunned. Finally, we sat up and quietly shared our wonderment. Then, spontaneously, we each wandered through the forest, touching the trees and gazing up into the forest cathedral.

Blindfold activities can be uniquely powerful in reawakening and exhilarating our minds and senses. Because sight is our dominant sense, when it is removed our other senses are heightened. The more heightened our sensory awareness, the more alive we feel.

BLIND WALK

Blind Walk is a simple yet profound activity. The leader guides his blindfolded partner along a route that has fascinating sensory stimuli—examples might be a gravelly beach, an overarching oak forest, a fern-populated ravine, or a windy ridge. When the pair approach something in nature of particular interest, the guide brings his partner over to experience it through touch, hearing, and smell. Their thoughts stilled by a flood of sensory impressions, players experience life more vividly.

SENSORY
AWARENESS,
TRUST

• Day / anywhere
• 2 or more people
• Ages 7 and up
• Blindfolds

To play, divide up in pairs, and make sure there's a responsible player for each team. Young children and adolescents can pair with an adult or a mature teenage guide. Explain to the players that the blindfolded partner is wholly dependent on the guide to keep him safe. Tell the guides *they* are the eyes for their partners.

Demonstrate how to comfortably lead a blindfolded player: Stand next to him, clasp his hand, and pin his forearm securely against your waist with your elbow bent. This position allows the guide to stay closely connected with the blindfolded player and to lead him gently. Guides should watch carefully for logs, rocks, low-lying branches, and other hazards.

BACK HOME

In *Back Home* the guide leads his blindfolded partner to a one-of-a-kind spot outdoors. Perhaps it is an area with a distinctive boulder and tree, or alongside a cascading stream banked with mossy rocks. (The blindfolded player should be able to explore the site comfortably and safely.) Players feel the texture and shape of the nearby rocks and plants, sense the presence of the sun and wind, and listen to the surrounding sounds. Before leaving the site, the guide can stimulate the blindfolded player's imagination and memory by asking him to visualize the area. Then the guide leads his partner back to the starting point, removes the blindfold, and asks his partner to find the spot by using his sensory memory.

EXPLORING,
ORIENTATION,
SENSORY
AWARENESS

• Day / anywhere
• 2 or more people
• Ages 10 and up
• Blindfolds

Encourage both players to remain silent while the blindfolded partner explores the special spot and walks to and from the area. Tell the players, "The more attentive you are with your blindfold on, the easier it will be for you to find your spot again with your eyes open."

Before leading *Back Home*, make sure the play area is free from poisonous plants, insects, and other hazards.

BLIND TRAIL

With imagination and forty to sixty yards of rope you can create a marvelous adventure for others. Find a clear area that contains a variety of intriguing features, such as older trees, lichen-covered boulders, a fallen log, and different microclimates. Choose a pathway that connects the site's most fascinating natural objects and places. Then string the rope along the pathway to guide the blindfolded players. Make sure there aren't any poisonous plants, insect nests, or rock crevices that might harbor snakes.

A typical urban park can also work well for *Blind Trail*. Walking with closed eyes heightens the senses and makes even a fairly simple trail enchanting.

SENSORY AWARENESS, TRUST
- Day / anywhere
- 2 or more people
- Ages 9 and up
- Rope, blindfolds

To start your *Blind Trail*, choose a sturdy tree and tie one end of the rope around it at the average waist height of the players. Then determine which side of the rope—left or right—the blindfolded players will walk on. Make sure that the side selected is free from low-lying limbs, rocks, and other obstacles.

From time to time change the waist-high level of the rope so that it goes, for example, underneath a rock or log, and thus forces players to explore objects on the ground. To keep the rope taut, tie it to a sturdy tree or other stable object at intervals. A taut rope will prevent blindfolded players from swinging off the intended pathway into trees or other obstacles. If the rope runs along the ground at points, use tent pegs to secure and tighten the line.

Some players will walk through the *Blind Trail* slowly, touching and feeling everything within arm's reach. Restless children, however, may be tempted to race through the trail. You can prolong their exploration, and help them to experience more, by winding the rope up the trunk of a tree, or stringing the rope through a tree's main fork. Placing natural objects with unique shapes and textures—such as a deer antler or mossy rock—along the trail will add variety and interest.

During *Blind Trail*, it's calming to create a long stretch where players can walk quietly, feel the warmth of the sun, listen to the chattering of birds, sense the ground beneath them, and hear the wind singing in the trees.

Suggestions for playing BLIND TRAIL:

- Choose four or more responsible helpers to manage the flow of the *Blind Trail* activity and to ensure player safety. Station one helper at the end of the trail and another one at the beginning. Designate two or more helpers to be spotters to aid trail walkers if necessary.

- So that players won't see the roped trail beforehand, gather your group a little distance away from the trail.

- Create a receptive mood for *Blind Trail* by first playing a quiet activity or by telling a calm story.

- Lead blindfolded players four at a time to the beginning of the blind trail by using the *Caterpillar Walk* (see page 139).

- If you want the player to walk on the left side of the rope, start him on the trail by having a helper place the player's right hand on the rope and telling him to stay always on the left side of the rope. The leader encourages the player to explore and experience as much as he can during his *Blind Trail* walk. After each player begins walking the trail, the leader should wait another twenty to thirty seconds before starting the next player in order to create a calm space around each player.

- Once players finish the trail they can sit quietly and observe other players still on the trail, or they can become spotters. When everyone has walked the trail blindfolded, lead the group around the trail again—now with eyes open.

GUIDED IMAGERY

Legend tells us that King Arthur's boyhood tutor, Merlin, was a great magician. Merlin knew that the lessons of life are best taught by nature. Using his wizard's power, he transformed Arthur into various animals—fish, hawk, ant, goose, and badger—so that he could experience important life lessons as each animal.

Guided imagery is a marvelous conduit for entering into the essence of another form of life. Experiencing another form of life intuitively in our hearts and minds, we find it easier to appreciate the special gifts of that life form.

When you create your own guided imagery, remember that the more deeply your listeners become absorbed in the images, the more clearly they'll remember the details. To give your story vividness and clarity, choose words and phrases that refer to the physical senses. When the stories you tell are rich with sights, sounds, tastes, and feelings, the information you weave into the story is retained for a long time. Allow plenty of time in your narration for the imagination to absorb each scene. Narrating to appropriate background music helps deepen the mood.*

To be truly effective, your imagery should have an expansive quality, so that it lifts the listener into the realm of noble thoughts and ideals.

Most scientists shy away from "anthropomorphism" and would say that trees lack self-awareness. On the other hand, many poets have attributed human feelings to trees. Much more important than who's

* For the guided visualization *Tree Imagery*, I've enjoyed using the following music: Beethoven's "Pastoral" Symphony #6, Vivaldi's *The Four Seasons*, and Pachelbel's "Canon in D."

right or wrong is *what do humans feel* when they "become" a tree and experience life as trees do.

In the imagery that follows, players imagine themselves to be a deciduous tree. The narrator describes how the tree's roots and branches reach out from the trunk, deep into the ground and high into the sky. A mature tree provides shelter for countless plants and animals. Trees moderate seasonal temperature extremes, and create a more supportive environment for all forest inhabitants. In fact, a single tree supports and nourishes a whole community of life forms. Living the life of a tree is a marvelous practice for broadening one's sympathies and sense of self.

When planning a guided imagery session, ask yourself what lessons or qualities one can learn from a particular plant, animal, or natural phenomenon. Then, in your imagery, give special care to bringing out these qualities.

One quality of trees that I especially admire is their inner strength. Trees can't run away from situations; they must stand firm and face the winter storms. While they patiently endure wind, lightning, and other hazards, their roots hold them firmly in place. In *Tree Imagery*, people feel what it's like to stand firm, to weather adversity, to draw strength from deeply planted roots. The analogy to human life is instructive, because the players learn to not let themselves be bowled over by tests and trials, but to reach down inside themselves for inner strength.

TREE IMAGERY

Tree Imagery is perhaps this book's most effective practice for instilling an ecological awareness and ethic. It's heartwarming to see participants "become" a tree, and fully immerse themselves in the life of the forest, beautifully expressing such noble qualities as benevolence and joyous harmony.

This activity can be practiced indoors or outdoors. To play outdoors, try to find a clear area under a large, deciduous tree.

Have the players stand with their eyes closed, near enough to you that they can easily hear you, and with a little space around each individual player. Tell them they're going to experience a year in the life of a deciduous tree.

While you narrate the imagery, the trees can choose to hold their arms up like branches, or simply to visualize their branches upraised. With younger children, moving their arm-branches helps channel their restlessness.

APPRECIATION OF TREES, FOREST BIOLOGY EMPATHY

• Day and night / anywhere, ideally near deciduous trees

• 2 or more people

• Ages 5 and up

• CD or MP3 music and player optional

You can read the visualization below, or use it as a framework for creating your own. With young children or groups with short attention spans, shorten your presentation by omitting secondary facts and curtailing some of your mood-setting description. Your skill with *Tree Imagery* will improve every time you lead it.

TREE IMAGERY *Narration*
Begin with the group standing under a tree.

Close your eyes.

Trees are very important to life on earth. They give the world much of its oxygen. They provide food, shelter, and a place of well-being for all forest life. They warm the winter air, and cool the summer air, thus creating an environment conducive to the healthy existence of all forest life. Trees inspire us with thoughts of beauty, strength, and serenity.

Stand with your feet shoulder-distance apart so that you have a feeling of strength and stability. Imagine a forest of trees in front of you—behind you—to your left—and to your right. As far as you can see—you are surrounded by trees.

Feel a large taproot dropping down through your legs and feet and going down deep into the earth. See the taproot descending one yard—two yards. Feel your taproot growing around—and through—the rocks, gripping you firmly into the earth.

Now, just beneath the surface of the soil, send out your lateral roots in an ever-widening circle—to ten feet—thirty feet—and beyond. At the tips of your lateral roots are tiny little root hairs. Feel your root hairs growing to cover every square inch of soil beneath you.

There is as much of you growing underground as there is in the sky above. Feel your roots holding you tall and upright in the sky. Gently sway back and forth.

Mentally look at your large trunk and see how big and round you are. Is your bark smooth or rough? Is it light-colored or dark? Follow your trunk up higher and higher until your branches begin to divide up and part, and spread out into the sky. Follow your branches as they become smaller and smaller—until you can see the very tips of your branches.

What kind of leaves do you have? Are they large and pointed? Or are they small and round?

It's summertime, the sun is warm, and the days are long. A light breeze blows through the forest, swaying your branches gently back and forth.

Extend your arms and feel all your leaves receiving the light of the sun. Feel your leaves turning sunlight and air into life. Bring into your leaves the nourishment you receive from the sun and pass it on to the rest of the tree. Feel the food you've made descending down your branches—to your trunk—and to your roots below.

Deep in the earth, draw in moisture with your tiny little root hairs. Feel the moisture gathering into tiny little steams—then merging as a river surging up your trunk—racing higher and higher—through your branches and leaves and out into the atmosphere. Continue to draw sustenance from the sun—feel it flowing through you. Give to the sky the water from the earth; permeate the surrounding air with moisture.

It's autumn now—the days are shorter and the sunlight less intense. Your life processes slow down, and you've stopped making food. The air is cooler, and the sap in your leaves descends from your branches to your trunk and to your roots below. Here food is stored to nourish next spring's growth.

As the sap withdraws from your leaves, they turn a vivid color. What color of leaves do *you* have: red—yellow—orange—or gold? Observe all your leaves, on all your branches, radiant with color. And look at the trees around you, clothed in their blazing autumn foliage.

Storm clouds roll over the horizon, darkening the sky. Gusts of wind push against your branches—raindrops patter on your leaves. A fierce wind now blows through the forest, tears off many of your leaves, and drives them to the ground. Gaze at the forest floor. See it covered with your leaves and with leaves from the trees all around you.

An even bigger storm blows in from the sea. Listen to its roar as it surges through the forest. Powerful gusts rattle your branches. Like a ship on an angry sea, you are tossed back and forth—back and forth. Only your large taproot and strong lateral roots keep you anchored in the earth.

The wind is slackening, and the storm has blown itself out. Your branches are bare and the ground is painted with gold, yellow, and red leaves. One by one, your last remaining leaves cast off and fall gently to the earth. The temperature drops, and snow begins to fall. Your dark silhouette stands sharply against the gray, somber, winter sky.

The winter forest is still and silent, and only a few brave birds can be heard. Many of the birds and mammals have left for warmer environments. You've died back to only one percent of your living tissue—retreating to a thin thread of life, just inside your bark.

Day after winter day you stand virtually lifeless. But stored in tiny buds are next year's leaves and flowers, covered by a waxy sheath protecting them from the wet and cold of winter. Kneel down, now, and become a tiny leaf bud. Ice may freeze around you, but you rest

 safe and secure, like a babe in its mother's womb, waiting for longer and warmer days.

With each passing day, the sun climbs higher in the sky, and spreads its warmth across the land. When the combination of longer and warmer days is just right, the sap stored in your roots races up your trunk to the very tips of your branches, awakening the tender, vibrant-green leaves.

Now, slowly rise and unfold as a tiny spring leaf. Grow large, grow green. Open completely to the spring sun and receive its life-giving rays. Bring the nourishment you feel down to the rest of the tree. Become all the leaves of the tree, and gather and pass on to the tree the energy and vitality you receive from the sun.

Spring is a time of incredible growth and renewal. 99 percent of your living tissue is restored. Your branch tips are reaching out and upwards. Your roots are once again flourishing in the earth. You're growing from both ends—and expanding just a little around your trunk.

Your renewal adds a tremendous vitality to the forest. Many animals have returned. Birds are landing on your branches. Reach out with one of your branches to let a songbird land on you. Flowering plants are pushing up and out from the earth, and deer and rabbits are grazing below you.

All forest creatures depend on you for food, shelter—and, yes, even a sense of well-being. John Muir said that there is "an essential Love, overlying, underlying, pervading all things." Spread your branches out to all those living in the forest and embrace them. Feel that you share one life together in beauty and harmony.

Facilitator: *Keep your eyes closed and lie down on your back. I will read a poem about the different parts of a tree.*

Roots going down,
reaching
through damp earth deep.
Down, down,
holding me here.

Open your eyes and look at the trunk and then the branches of a large tree.

My great round trunk,
massive and slender,
solid yet yielding,
carrier of life.

My long limbs
stretching out for space,
tips tickled by the wind,
touched by the sun.

All forest creatures
take shelter
within me, beneath me.

Roots anchored deep,
limbs lofty high,
I abide in both worlds
of earth and sky.

As the participants continue lying down, gazing at overarching tree limbs, the facilitator reads the following quotation:

> *My heart is tuned to the quietness*
> *that the stillness of nature inspires.*
> —Hazrat Inayat Khan

The facilitator continues:

Could all the trees in the forest sit up now. Think of three words or phrases that best describe your experience of being a tree. One at a time, when you're ready, please say aloud your words and/or phrases.

It's beautiful to hear participants describe being a tree, experiencing the four seasons, interacting with other forest creatures, and feeling the energy of life flowing through their bodies. Below are some of the words that participants often share:

Resilient   Joyful   Rejuvenating

Cyclical   Nurturing   Peaceful   Interconnected

Harmony   Powerful   Flowing with Change

Wholeness   Vitality   Healing

SHARE
INSPIRATION
Activities

The activities in this section bring to the surface a group's shared experiences and feelings. Through song, story, and art, they help us celebrate nature.

t was sundown, and the group and I sat overlooking a vast marsh teeming with birds. For a long time we watched the sun setting. After it had disappeared

below the horizon, we played the pantomime activity, *Special Moments*, to honor and celebrate our day together.

Susie, a twelve-year-old girl, walked to the top of the levee, turned toward us, and clasped her hands above her head, holding her arms in a circle.

She smiled for a moment, and then walked slowly backward down the other side of the levee. The perfection of her rendition of the sun setting touched everyone, reminding us of the beautiful moment we'd shared.

SPECIAL MOMENTS

During an extend-ed program, group members often experience sublime moments with nature. This activity brings these shared—but often unexpressed—memories out into the open, reinforcing people's appreciation of nature and of one another.

GROUP BONDING
- Day and night / anywhere
- For 10 or more people
- Ages 11 and up
- No supplies

Gather the group into a circle and ask partici-pants to think of inspiring or humorous events that took place during their time together. Ask for volunteers who would like to act out their special moments—each volunteer individually performing one event.

Tell the group to make their sharings simple and silent. After an event has been mimed, the audience waits for the sharer to quietly explain the incident. Often shared smiles or laugh-ter indicate that no explanation is necessary. The leader can start things rolling by being the first to act out a special moment.

Groups have enjoyed acting out such events as observing a special animal, enjoying a magical sunrise, sharing a silent walk, and having a humorous moment with another participant.

NATURE REFLECTIONS

Deep in the woods of Great Smoky Mountains National Park, we were on a tiny island with water rushing by on one side and a serene pond on the other—a magical place, perfect for *Nature Reflections*. The fifty people in our group were absorbed in the beauty surrounding us. Some were sitting on rocks in the stream; others were under the trees, gazing across the pond. Everyone was calm and wholly attentive. Each of us had selected a card on which were printed an inspiring thought and a nature meditation that we could use to focus our awareness. It was heart-warming to see such a sincere desire to draw inspiration from the natural world. Even though our group was so large, there was a remarkable mood of silent communion with nature. Later, we shared our experiences and insights. *Nature Reflections* is an excellent exercise for extending a contemplative mood and encouraging deep sharing among participants.

To play *Nature Reflections*, you'll need to collect a number of inspiring quotations and write them on index cards, one saying per card. Each thought can have accompanying activity text to direct the reader to a personal experience of nature. Avoid quotations that are abstract and mental; you want to help participants be in their *hearts*, not in their minds.

You can find thought-provoking quotations in my books *Listening to Nature* and *The Sky and Earth Touched Me*. The *Sharing Nature Online Resource* website also has downloadable *Nature Reflection* cards.

The following quotations and accompanying exercises are from *Listening to Nature*:

REFLECTING ON THE WORDS OF GREAT NATURALISTS

- Day and night / natural area
- For 1 person or more
- Ages 15 and up
- Quotation cards

1.

When in the wilds, we must not carry
our problems with us or the joy is lost.

—Sigurd Olson

Mark Twain was once asked if he would like to go on a vacation. He replied, "I'd be glad to, if only I didn't have to take that fella, Mark Twain, with me." Like Mark Twain, we often take "that fella" along with us when we go outdoors for recreation. Our problems, worries, and mental baggage all tag along with us. When you go into nature, leave your everyday plans and concerns behind. Freeing yourself in this way will allow you to experience nature's rejuvenating power.

2.

My heart is tuned
to the quietness
that the stillness of
nature inspires.

—H. I. Khan

Find a quiet place and listen to the sounds around you. *Listen also for the silences between sounds.* When your mind wanders, repeat the above saying to help bring you back to the present moment.

3.

Holy Earth Mother, the trees and all nature
are witnesses of your thoughts and deeds.

—Winnebago Prayer

Invisible Spirit has become visible through all the myriad forms of nature. As you go for a walk, mentally repeat this Winnebago prayer of reverence for the earth and its Creator. When an animal, a plant, a rock, or a beautiful scene draws your attention, stop, and silently offer thanks to the Creator for the joy and beauty you feel.

HOW TO PLAY: Find a quiet, captivating place where each player can be alone. A beautiful setting will bring the quotations to life and inspire the group's idealism. Place the quotation cards face down and let each player choose a card. Tell players that if they don't resonate with the ones chosen, they can look for another one. Allow about ten minutes for reflection, then call the group back, have them sit in a circle, and ask them to share their experiences with their individual quotations.

FOLDING POEM

Folding Poem beautifully captures the inspiration from shared nature experiences. This activity was created by the North Carolina Outward Bound School.*

TO PLAY: Divide your group into teams of three or four, and give each team a pencil and paper. Each team will create a poem expressing their experience during, for example, a week in the wilderness or a *Tree Imagery* visualization, or on seeing a special animal. Below are the directions for creating a *Folding Poem*:

1. Person A writes the first line of the poem and passes the paper to B.

2. Person B responds to A's line by writing two lines for the poem, then folds the paper so that C sees only the second line written by B.

3. Person C responds to the line written by B by writing two additional lines. C folds the paper so that A sees only the second line written by C.

4. Person A writes the last line of the poem based on the second line of poetry written by C.

FELLOWSHIP
REFLECTION

- Day and night / anywhere
- For 3 or more people
- Ages 10 and up
- Pencils, paper

As the poem is being written, each player has only a partial knowledge of the poem. But the beauty of this activity is that—because of the shared group experience—the poems created have a wonderful continuity and life to them.

* Larry Crenshaw and the North Carolina Outward Bound School, *EarthBook* (Birmingham, AL: Menasha Ridge Press, 1995).

When all the teams are finished (about 10 minutes), have each team read their poem.

Lines of poetry written by team players A, B, and C

A _____

B _____

— — — — — — FOLD — — — — — —

B _____

C _____

— — — — — — FOLD — — — — — —

C _____

A _____

You can write a *Folding Poem* with any number of players by passing the poem around to everyone so that each one can see only the last line written. Then you can have the person who started the poem also end it, as above.

SILENT SHARING WALK

On *Silent Sharing Walks* participants stroll serenely through beautiful natural areas. In groups of two or three, they walk slowly and silently, communing with nature's wonders. The harmony they experience during this exercise opens their hearts to all creation.

One evening at dusk, in a mountain forest in Southern California, twelve teenage boys and I experienced a magical *Silent Sharing Walk*. We walked slowly down a forest track that overlooked the great Mojave Desert. The electrified silence vibrated with insect and bird song. When a walker saw something captivating, he tapped the shoulder of the nearest boy, and pointed to whatever he had noticed.

We spotted a doe, calmly browsing our way. When we arrived within thirty feet of the deer, she raised her head and serenely gazed at us. Her innocent, trusting manner touched us deeply—we felt completely accepted by this gentle forest native.

Later, three coyotes came trotting toward us. They were as curious as puppies, coming a few feet closer, then stopping and howling as they watched us, tipping their heads from side to side, wondering what were these silent strangers.

RAPPORT WITH NATURE, EMPATHY
- Day sunset / anywhere
- For 2 or more people
- Ages 10 and up
- No supplies

During *Silent Sharing Walks*, animals feel our state of mind and our peaceful, harmonious intent. In silence, we feel a common bond with the rest of life and sense the One that flows through all.

Even during short, mid-day *Silent Sharing Walks*, players can enter, for a time, a magical and loving world.

DIRECTIONS: The ideal number for a *Silent Sharing Walk* is two or three walkers. If the group is larger, divide into sharing teams of two or three people.

Tell the participants to walk in silence. When one walker sees something captivating, instead of speaking aloud about it, he should gently tap the shoulder of one or more teammates, then point to the object and silently share the enjoyment.

Choose an attractive trail or open area that's easy to wander through. Since sharing teams move slowly, the distance they travel won't be great. If there are several sharing teams, agree on a time and place to gather afterwards.

Silent Sharing Walkers experience a beautiful rapport among themselves and with nature. Keeping silent and sharing nonverbally, the walkers become fully present with nature and with one another. It is moving to observe the serene, childlike love of the walkers as they gather around newly discovered flora, bird nests, and other natural wonders.

WITH BEAUTY BEFORE ME

This activity helps players feel a sense of oneness with all living things.

SEEING BEAUTY EVERYWHERE

• Day / anytime
• For 1 person or more
• Ages 14 and up
• CD or MP3 music and player optional

HOW TO PLAY: Walk slowly and repeat the poem below. Enjoy the beauty of the clouds, grasses, trees, and hills, and whatever else comes to your attention. Among the Navajo, the word "beauty" means "harmony." When you say the word "beauty" in each line, feel a sense of harmony in everything you see.

> **With beauty before me,**
> *May I walk.*
>
> **With beauty behind me,**
> *May I walk.*
>
> **With beauty above me,**
> *May I walk.*
>
> **With beauty below me,**
> *May I walk.*
>
> **With beauty all around me,**
> *May I walk.*
>
> **Wandering on a trail of beauty,**
> *Lively, I walk.*
>
> —*Navajo Chant*

For a group walk, you can have players, before starting out, listen to and sing the *With Beauty Before Me* song.*

* A recording of the "With Beauty Before Me" song is available through *Sharing Nature Online Resources* (see page 191).

RECIPE FOR A FOREST

If you could create your own forest, what would it look like? This activity helps children think about sustainability and beauty with an imaginative spirit.

Tell the children each one now owns one square mile of land in which to make a dream forest. Tell the players, "Because your forest needs to sustain itself year after year, it needs such essential ingredients as healthy soil, water, sunlight, trees, fungus, bacteria, ground cover, and animals."

INTERDEPENDENCE
SUSTAINABILITY
IMAGINATION
• Day / anytime
• 2 or more people
• Ages 7 and up
• Pencils, index cards

Encourage the children to create a forest that is not only sustainable but beautiful. In their woodland they can have colorful birds, old growth trees, people who love the forest, cloudbursts, perpetual rainbows—anything they want.

After the children have listed their ingredients, they can draw a picture of their forest and share it with the group. *Recipe for a Forest* is an excellent follow-up to the experiential tree activities in this book.

A LETTER TO MYSELF

Magical moments of deep connection with nature and with others should be remembered forever. But it's easy to forget our intention to live life more meaningfully. This exercise captures the immediacy of people's inspiration in a letter they write to themselves. One month later, this letter is mailed to them to remind them of life's higher priorities.

This activity has two worthwhile effects: Writing the letter impresses the experience and its lessons on the player's mind, and receiving the letter reinforces his intention to live more closely with nature.

Close a several-days-long inspirational program, by asking participants to write a letter to themselves, and to enclose the letter in a self-addressed mailing envelope. The writers tell themselves what they're feeling now and what they want to remember from this time of connection with nature. Tell participants that no one else will read their letters and that their letters will be mailed in one month.

One woman shared with me the letter she wrote after attending a nature tour my wife and I had led to the American Southwest:

APPRECIATION
IDEALISM
- Day and night / anywhere
- For 1 person or more
- Ages 13 and up
- Writing paper, pen(s), mailing envelopes(s)

177

To myself:

"I have had a wonderful time these past ten days enjoying and experiencing nature. My most moving experience was hiking the Lower Calf Creek Falls Trail. Walking alone with no other member of the group in sight, I looked up at the enormous walls of the canyon and truly felt a divine presence. The strength, grandeur, and timelessness of the walls of the canyon were profound for me. I felt guided into the waterfall by these great walls. I want to keep the memories of this trip with me always—to give me calmness, so I can feel nature in my everyday activities and not lose the feelings of closeness to a greater presence."

Yours truly, Diane

MY LETTER

Date: _____

_____

_____

_____

_____

_____

_____

_____

_____

_____

_____

_____

_____

_____

_____

_____

_____

_____

STORYTELLING TO SHARE INSPIRATION

When John Muir told stories of his encounters with wild animals, trees, and mountain storms, his audiences felt they were actually there. One listener exclaimed, "Our foreheads felt the wind and the rain!" As mentioned earlier, storytelling is a shared brain experience.

Listeners actually live the story. MRI scans show that storyteller and audience have the same neurological activity in the insula, a frontal brain region that fosters self-awareness and feeling. When we tell uplifting stories about the lives of great naturalists, everyone (including the teller) benefits emotionally and spiritually.

In this time of enormous challenges, it's crucial that we offer wholesome role models. "A nation is known by the men and women its own people look up to as great," said a wise man. In modern cultures, young people universally revere celebrities in sports, music, and movies. How different to share the noble lives of men and women who have deeply resonated with the earth and cared for its inhabitants—when we do so, we are looking to heroes truly worth emulating. As we relive the life experiences and worldviews of such people as John Muir, Rachel Carson, and Henry David Thoreau, we are touched and transformed.

CONSERVATION
HISTORY, IDEALISM,
DELIGHT IN NATURE
- Day and night / anywhere
- For 2 or more people
- Ages 4 and up
- Costumes, props

Choose a person whose life inspires you, and whose life and message have pioneered new ways of living and being. Because you yourself are inspired, you'll be able to pour sincere enthusiasm into your presentation. From your character's life select funny and exciting stories, as well as inspirational nature experiences. Arrange your stories according to the following moods—funny, exciting, and dramatic, then deeply meaningful—to ensure an enthusiastic and receptive audience.

For special impact, you can memorize short, resounding passages of your character's words. If, however, you try to memorize all of your lines, your performance may feel stilted. Concentrate instead on remembering the story's main points, scene by scene. Knowing the key parts will help you relax, be spontaneous, and have fun telling the story. The more you're in the joy of the story, the more effective your presentation will be.

I've heard that the Navajo discipline their children through storytelling. If a young child behaves badly, instead of confronting him about his conduct, adults will tell a story about a child of the same age who acted in the same way. Since children love stories, they listen with full attention. As he lives the story through the other child, the misbehaving child sees the consequences of his actions. I can imagine the listening child's eyes growing large and thoughtful—as one often sees during storytelling—and the words "I'll never do that!" coming into his mind.

Modern storytellers too can convey a gentle, loving, and winning message to audiences of all ages. Telling stories about uplifting men and women is one of the best ways to communicate the higher values that are so needed in the world today.

Joseph Cornell has created a living history program on the life of John Muir, and his book, *John Muir: My Life with Nature*, is an excellent storytelling resource.

Eleven Tips for Effective Storytelling

1. Use simple props, such as a hat. Props help transport the audience to another time and place.

2. Create (and learn) a strong beginning and ending. Doing so will help you start confidently and finish strongly.

3. Because people won't remember so much the words of your story as the feeling of it, missing a few lines of your story won't matter. If you do forget what comes next, don't panic. Pause, and keep eye contact with the audience. The more relaxed you are, the easier it will be to remember the forgotten point, and recover gracefully.

4. Include humor. It relaxes the audience and makes them open and receptive to your message. The best time to make a serious point is often right after a humorous statement.

5. Vary your speech, rhythm, and mood. Changing pace keeps your performance lively and interesting. Pauses allow listeners to rest, catch up, and digest key points.

6. Actors use a technique called "emotional recall" to energize their performances. To use this technique, summon a past memory to trigger the emotion you need to express for the story.

7. If you're playing more than one character, change your voice and personality to fit each one. The key is to change your consciousness so that you can feel the reality of your character. The audience will believe you to the degree that you believe in the character.

8. Use your hands to create space and dimension, or to paint a picture. Use gestures to embellish and punctuate your points. Make gestures large and away from the body, so that people sitting in the back can see them.

9. Pause for emphasis and suspense; calm control will also enable you to give each word the richness it deserves.

10. Adapt your performance for different age groups. Children think in physical and visual terms; adults are more interested in the ideas and meaning of a story.

11. Think of *sharing with* your audience, instead of *performing for* them. Offer listeners the delight you feel for the story and for the privilege of connecting heart to heart with them.

THE BIRDS
OF THE AIR

Because it brings
people together to celebrate
their oneness with all living
things, *The Birds of the Air* is a marvelous way to conclude a nature
outing. The song's beautiful melody and lyrics are accompanied by
simple, graceful movements uniting body, mind, and heart.

Once during a lecture at Taipei City Hall, I led four hundred Taiwanese in *The Birds of the Air*. When the Taiwanese began making the song's motions with flowing, Tai Chi-inspired movements, the exquisite interplay of music and grace overwhelmed me.

This exercise awakens and amplifies people's love for the earth and thereby fosters a feeling of stewardship. By expressing gratitude to nature, we invite her reciprocal response. Many times birds have responded to groups singing *The Birds of the Air* by flying to the nearby trees and singing exuberantly.

EXPRESSING LOVE
FOR NATURE

• **Day / night**
• **For 1 person or more**
• **Ages 5 and up**
• **Musical instrument, or CD / MP3 player**

Here are the words (in bold) and accompanying arm motions:

 ### The birds of the air are my brothers,

Stretch the arms out to the sides, turning the palms down.
Gracefully wave the arms as if they were bird wings.

All flowers my sisters,

Bring the palms together in front of you, then spread
your fingers apart like a flower opening.

The trees are my friends.

Join the palms together above your head and
sway your body like the trunk of a tree.

All living creatures,

Stretch your arms out to the sides in welcome to all creatures.

Mountains,

Bring your fingertips together at chin level to form a mountain peak.

And streams,

Keeping your left hand at the chin, sweep your right arm
out to the side, fluttering the fingers like rippling water.

I take unto my care.

Cup one hand on top of the other, palms up,
at heart level, holding all nature in your care.

For this green earth is our Mother,

Sweep your hands up and out from the heart,
reaching out to include the whole earth.

Hidden in the sky is the Spirit above.

Look upward, extending your arms toward the sky.

I share one Life with all who are here;

Cross your hands at the heart.

To everyone I give my love,

Keep the right hand at your heart, and sweep
the left hand out to the side with the palm up.

To everyone I give my love.

Keep the left hand out to the side, and sweep
the right hand out to the other side, with palm up.

To share this exercise, go to a place where natural beauty stimulates the group's higher feelings. Form a line or half circle with the participants facing a pleasing direction. Stand in front of the group, and repeat the words to the song while you demonstrate the arm motions. As you say each line or phrase, feel its meaning and project those feelings out to your surroundings. For example, while saying, "The trees are my friends," feel your closeness with the trees.

Tell everyone to concentrate on sending to nature thoughts of love and goodwill. Then sing or play *The Birds of the Air* song, inviting everyone to join in. (You can watch a video demonstration of *The Birds of the Air* at www.sharenature.org. The song is available on this website and also on the Sharing Nature Audio Resources CD; the musical score is in the appendix on page 196.)

PAGE 3 | John Hendrickson Photography **7** | Sharing Nature Worldwide Photographs, Japan **9** | Sharing Nature Worldwide Photographs, Brazil **15** | Heart of Nature Photography (Robert Frutos) **16** | George Beinhorn **17** | George Beinhorn **18** | Argentina National Parks National Library **19** | Photographer Unknown **20–21** | Heart of Nature Photography (Robert Frutos) **22** | John Hendrickson Photography **25** | Joyful Photography (Barbara Bingham) **26** | Heart of Nature Photography (Robert Frutos) **27** | Maya Khosla, India **28** | *above:* Snowland Great River Environmental Assoc. of Qing Hai, China | *below:* OLS Adventure Club, Uganda **29** | *above:* Sharing Nature Worldwide Photographs, Japan | *below:* Joyful Photography (Barbara Bingham) **30** | *above:* Sharing Nature Worldwide Photographs, Japan | *below:* Sharing Nature Worldwide Photographs **33** | Sharing Nature Worldwide Photographs, Portugal **35** | Nanne Wienands, Germany **36** | Sharing Nature Worldwide Photographs, New Zealand **37** | Jenny Coxon Photography **40** | John Hendrickson Photography **42** | Sharing Nature Worldwide Photographs, Portugal **43** | Sharing Nature Worldwide Photographs, Taiwan **44** | Agnes Meijs, www.natuurlijkheden.nl **46** | Sharing Nature Worldwide Photographs, Portugal **47** | OLS Adventure Club, Uganda **48–49** | John Hendrickson Photography **50** | Sharing Nature Worldwide Photographs, Japan **52** | OLS Adventure Club, Uganda **53** | *above:* Nanne Wienands, Germany | *middle:* Sharing Nature Worldwide Photographs, Japan | *below:* Sharing Nature Worldwide Photographs, Brazil **55** | Dr. Gertrude Hein, Germany **56** | Dr. Gertrude Hein, Germany **57** | Sharing Nature Worldwide Photographs, Japan **58** | *above:* Sharing Nature Worldwide Photographs, Brazil | *below:* Joyful Photography (Barbara Bingham) **59** | Snowland Great River Environmental Assoc. of Qing Hai, China **60** | *above:* Bruce Malnor | *below:* Sharing Nature Worldwide Photographs, Portugal **61** | Dr. Gertrude Hein, Germany **62** | Sharing Nature Worldwide Photographs **63** | Original: St. Regis Paper Company; adapted and modified by Peter Kolb, Montana State Extension Forestry **64** | Sharing Nature Worldwide Photographs, Japan **65** | Dr. Gertrude Hein, Germany **66** | *above:* Sharing Nature Worldwide Photographs | *below:* Sharing Nature Worldwide Photographs, Japan **67** | Sharing Nature Worldwide Photographs **68** | *above and below:* Sharing Nature Worldwide Photographs, Portugal **69** | *above:* Sharing Nature Worldwide Photographs, Portugal | *below:* John Hendrickson Photography **70** | *above:* Sharing Nature Worldwide Photographs, Portugal | *below:* Sharing Nature Worldwide Photographs **71** | Sharing Nature Worldwide Photographs **72** | *above:* Gert Olsson Photography / inNature West | *below:* John Hendrickson Photography **73** | Sharing Nature Worldwide Photographs **74** | Jenny Coxon Photography **75** | Jenny Coxon Photography **76** | John Hendrickson Photography **77** | John Hendrickson Photography **78** | Kirk Geisier / Shutterstock **79** | Gillmar / Shutterstock **80** | *above:* Sharing Nature Worldwide Photographs | *below:* OLS Adventure Club, Uganda **81** | Sharing Nature Worldwide Photographs, Brazil **82** | Sharing Nature Worldwide Photographs **83** | Heart of Nature Photography (Robert Frutos) **84** | *above:* Dr. Gertrude Hein, Germany | *below:* Dr. Gertrude Hein, Germany **85** | Sandi Croan Photography **86** | Joyful Photography (Barbara Bingham) **87** | Joyful Photography (Barbara Bingham) **88** | Jenny Coxon Photography **89** | Sharing Nature Worldwide Photographs, Japan **90** | Jenny Coxon Photography **92** | Sharing Nature Worldwide Photographs, Japan **93** | Joyful Photography (Barbara Bingham) **95** | OLS Adventure Club, Uganda **96** | *Aspen:* John Hendrickson Photography | *man:* Sharing Nature Worldwide Photographs, Taiwan **97** | *above:* John Hendrickson Photography | *below:* Sharing Nature Worldwide Photographs **98** | Joyful Photography (Barbara Bingham) **99** | John Hendrickson Photography **100** | Sharing Nature Worldwide Photographs **101** | 2009fotofriends / Shutterstock **102** | *above:* Hogs555 / CC-BY-SA-3.0 (modified) | *below:* John Hendrickson Photography **103** | Sharing Nature

"Give others the gift of joy, serenity,
and the feeling of wholeness. Take them
to the forest or seashore and let them
experience in focused ways the awe and
exuberance of the natural world."

—Joseph Cornell

Sharing Nature
ONLINE RESOURCES

To help you share nature with others, we've created the *Online Resources* page: here you can download and print activity handouts, game materials, and additional instructional aids. For a nominal fee you can access the following:

- Printable PDF handouts for fifteen activities;
- 120 printable Animal Clue Game Cards for 20 animals;
- Nature Reflections quotation cards;
- An MP3 of the song "With Beauty Before Me"; *and*
- An MP3 of "The Birds of the Air" song, and a video of that song with accompanying arm movements.

www.sharenature.org

Ideal for Parents with Young Children

Noses (**56**) • Wild Animal Scramble (**58**) • Animal Parts (**80**) • Guess and Run! Version II (**90**) • Sounds (**98**) • Colors (**99**) • Sound Map (**106**) • Camouflage Trail (**108**) • Micro-Hike (**112**) • Duplication (**113**) • Interview with Nature (**121**) • Camera (**125**) • Bird Calling (**129**) • Mystery Animal (**131**) • Meet a Tree (**137**) • The Birds of the Air (**184**)

Science and Natural History

Noses (**56**) • Wild Animal Scramble (**58**) • Build a Tree (**60**) • Natural Processes (**66**) • Owl and Crows (**68**) • Bat and Moth (**70**) • Predator-Prey (**72**) • Pyramid of Life (**74**) • Animal Clue Game (**81**) • Mystery Animal (**131**) • Sunset Watch (**146**) • Tree Imagery (**157**)

Indoors and Rainy Days

Getting Acquainted (**55**) • Noses (**56**) • Wild Animal Scramble (**58**) • Build a Tree (**60**) • Natural Processes (**66**) • Bat and Moth (**70**) • Predator-Prey (**72**) • Pyramid of Life (**74**) • Sled Dogs (**77**) • Animal Parts (**80**) • Animal Clue Game (**81**) • Noah's Ark (**86**) • Animals, Animals! (**110**) • Mystery Animal (**131**) • Vertical Poem (**144**) • Tree Imagery (**157**) • Special Moments (**167**) • Folding Poem (**171**) • Recipe for a Forest (**176**) • A Letter to Myself (**177**) • Storytelling to Share Inspiration (**180**) • The Birds of the Air (**184**)

Specifically for Teenagers or Adults

Getting Acquainted (**55**) • Sled Dogs (**77**) • I Am Curious About (**95**) • How Close? (**102**) • Tree Imagery (**157**) • Nature Reflections (**168**) • Folding Poem (**171**) • With Beauty before Me (**175**) • A Letter to Myself (**177**)

THE BIRDS OF THE AIR

words by Joseph Cornell, *music by* Michael Starner-Simpson

The birds of the air are my bro - thers,   All   flow-ers my sis-ters, the

trees are my friends.   All liv-ing crea- tures, mountains and streams,

I take un - to my   care.   For this green earth is our   mo - ther,

hid-den in the sky is the   spi - rit a - bove.

I share one life wi - ith all who are here; to ev-ry-one I give my

love,   to ev - ry-one I give my   love.

1. I prefer to eat insects but also eat sap, fruit, nuts, and berries.

2. Unlike most of my kind, I don't sing.

3. My average body temperature is 105°F.

4. I have four toes: the first and fourth face backward and the second and third face forward.

5. I have two long feathers, which provide balance when I fly or perch.

6. I can peck up to 20 times a second.

7. I use my strong bill to chisel wood. My long sticky tongue allows me to get my food deep inside the hole I've made in a tree.

VNNCODBJDQ

---

1. I am a true omnivore. I eat rodents, rabbits, insects, fruit, and eggs.

2. Males, females, and older offspring of my kind care for the young. Typically we live in a small family group.

3. A surprising number of my kind live in cities.

4. I dig a den for use during the winter. This den may be used over a number of generations.

5. I am cunning.

6. Our females are called vixens.

7. I have a very bushy tail, which can be red. I am a member of the dog family.

ENW

1. I have a heart, lungs, and kidneys just like you.

2. I don't have a bladder—so, when I have to go, I have to go right now!

3. The gland at the base of my tail secretes an oil that I use to coat my feathers. This coating protects me from the rain.

4. I eat anything I can catch: mice, small birds, lizards, and insects.

5. My bones are lightweight and some people describe them as "hollow," but actually they have inner struts that make them very strong.

6. My eyesight is eight times better than a human's. My sharp vision is very useful when I hunt at night.

7. The feathers on the top of my head are often mistaken for ears—but they are just feathers.

8. The food I cannot digest I regurgitate as a pellet. Most of my kind hoot at night.

NVK

---

1. As an adult, I look *nothing* like I did while I was young.

2. In my larval form, I breathe thru my anus.

3. You can find me near or in water.

4. My kind live for one to three years as aquatic larvae, and for usually a few months as an adult.

5. My prehistoric ancestors had large wingspans—up to 2½' long. Now the largest of us has a wingspan of only 7½" across.

6. I am an excellent flyer. I can fly up to 36mph. I can move my two sets of wings independently and I can fly in all directions.

7. My vision is exceptional! I have two large compound eyes which give me 360 degree vision. I can see a broader spectrum of colors

than humans can. Like a butterfly, I can be almost any color of the rainbow.

8. I have a long, slender body and just below my mouth are my six legs, which can form a basket to catch prey. I have four transparent wings. At rest I hold them out horizontally.

CQZFNMEKX

1. I'll eat almost anything: fruit, flower blossoms, nuts, snails, and slugs.

2. I am quite social and may live with eight or more of my kind.

3. Many animals like to eat me: snakes, raccoons, owls, and sometimes domestic cats.

4. I have large eyes that help me see at night, when I'm usually active.

5. I build a nest in trees and cover it with leaves and other forest materials.

6. I have fur and feed milk to my young.

7. Stretched between my forelegs and my hind legs is a membrane that lets me glide in midair. I don't actually fly, but I can glide as far as 150 feet between trees.

EKXHMF RPTHQQDK

1. Everyone in my family is a predator.

2. Some of my kind have been known to eat birds.

3. I don't have great eyesight, even though I have many eyes. I use my sense of touch to hunt.

4. Before I can eat my prey, I must turn it into a liquid by expelling stomach fluid on its body.

5. My kind live in funnels, sheets, tangles, or orbs. Others roam, without a home.

6. I have eight legs and fangs that inject venom.

7. From my body, I can produce silk, which is the strongest natural material on earth.

ROHCDQ

---

1. I am a modern day relative of the dinosaurs.

2. When a group of my kind is gathered, it is called a "siege."

3. I have long thin toes: one toe points backward and three toes point forward.

4. My feathers are soft. They can be blue, brown, black, white, or gray.

5. If you want to find me, look for water.

6. My wingspan is twice the length of my body. The largest of my kind have a wingspan of 66 to 79 inches.

7. I have a harpoon-shaped bill, which can easily grab fish, snakes, mice, frogs, amphibians, or invertebrates.

8. My neck is long and snake-like. I have long legs and you usually see me standing motionless, waiting for prey to come close.

GDQNM

ACKNOWLEDGEMENTS

I am grateful to Richard Louv, co-founder of the Children & Nature Network, for his outstanding work in promoting children in nature and for his thoughtful foreword and support. Thanks also to my friend of many years, Cheryl Charles, past president and co-founder of C&NN. Their efforts to connect children and families with nature have inspired and impacted countless lives in North America and abroad.

I would like to offer heartfelt thanks and deep appreciation to Anandi, my wife, who, since we met, has played an instrumental role in every book I've written. Anandi's clarity, editorial skill, and understanding of my work have been a Godsend.

Both Anandi and my colleague, Greg Traymar, read the manuscript numerous times and made many valuable suggestions. I so appreciate the creativity, deep understanding, and initiative Greg brings to the Sharing Nature work. Thanks to Alan Heubert and Susan Sanford for their helpful suggestions, and to Nicole Smith, who wrote the Animal Clues in Appendix D.

I would like also to express heartfelt appreciation to Jim Van Cleave, and Richard Salva of Crystal Clarity Publishers, for their editorial expertise and devotion to this project, and to Skip Barrett, my publisher and friend, for his vision and support.

Sharing Nature®
WORLDWIDE

THE NATURE AWARENESS WORK
of Joseph Bharat Cornell

oseph Cornell is an internationally renowned author and founder of Sharing Nature Worldwide, one of the planet's most widely respected nature awareness programs. His first book, *Sharing Nature with Children*, "sparked a worldwide revolution in nature education" and has been published in twenty languages and sold half a million copies. He is the honorary president of Sharing Nature Association of Japan, which has 10,000 members and 35,000 trained leaders.

He the author of the Sharing Nature Book Series, used by millions of parents, educators, naturalists, and youth and religious leaders all over the world. Mr. Cornell's books, *Listening to Nature* and *The Sky and Earth Touched Me*, have inspired thousands of adults to deepen their relationship with nature.

The U.S. Fish & Wildlife Service selected Mr. Cornell's *Sharing Nature with Children* as one of the fifteen most influential books published since 1890 for connecting children and families to nature. His highly effective outdoor learning strategy, Flow Learning™, was featured by the U.S. National Park Service as one of five recommended learning theories, along with the works of Maria Montessori, Howard Gardner, John Dewey, and Jean Piaget.

Mr. Cornell has received many international awards for his Sharing Nature books and work. He received the prestigious Countess Sonja-Bernadotte Prize in Germany for his vast influence on environmental education in Central Europe. In 2011 Cornell was selected as one of the world's "100 most influential opinion leaders committed to the Environment" by the French organization, Les Anges Gardiens de la Planète.

Known for his warmth and joyful enthusiasm, Cornell "has a genius for finding the essence of a subject, explaining it in clear and compelling ways, and then giving the reader creative exercises to gain an actual experience."

Joseph and his wife, Anandi, are senior ministers and residents of Ananda Village, in Northern California.

For more information about Joseph Cornell's books and activities visit: **www.jcornell.org**

SHARING NATURE
WELLNESS PROGRAM

 ohn Muir said, "Nature's peace flows into us as sunshine flows into trees." Nature, the great healer, offers gifts of joyful serenity and vitality to every receptive heart.

During a Sharing Nature Wellness program you'll practice nature exercises to quiet your mind and open your heart to all creation. You will learn how to internalize your experience of nature and feel more at peace with life.

You'll delight in joyful nature awareness activities, feel more positive and affirmative, and enjoy a spirit of community and communion with others and with nature. Nature's benevolent presence will remind you of life's higher priorities.

SHARING THE JOY OF NATURE SINCE 1979

Sharing Nature is a worldwide movement dedicated to helping children and adults deepen their relationship with nature. We offer training workshops, keynote presentations, online resources, webinars, and books to help people feel closer to nature and to others. Our Wellness programs provide uplifting experiences and healing for individuals, and for leaders in business, education, religion, and the public sector.

Sharing Nature coordinators are represented in numerous countries around the world and would be happy to speak to your group or organization. Our coordinators are exceptional individuals who love nature and people, and can bring them beautifully together.

We would love to hear from you. Please contact us to learn more about our offerings around the world.

Sharing Nature Worldwide

14618 Tyler Foote Road   Phone: (530) 478-7650
Nevada City, CA 95959   info@sharingnature.com

OTHER BOOKS BY JOSEPH CORNELL

The Sky and Earth Touched Me
Sharing Nature® Wellness Exercises

Written for adults desiring a deeper connection with nature, this book takes the Sharing Nature exercises to a higher level, and offers a transformative guide for healing and well-being in nature.

There is a tremendous power in these activities. One moment of touching nature can inspire you for a lifetime. Practicing these simple exercises will immerse you in the natural world and open your heart to all creation.

"Enriching, awakening, and life-changing nature experiences."

—**Roderic Knowles,** Founder of Living Tree Educational Foundation, author of *Gospel of the Living Tree*

Listening to Nature
How to Deepen Your Awareness of Nature

The beloved and bestselling book *Listening to Nature* will open your eyes and your heart to the peace and joyous spirit of the natural world. Joseph Bharat Cornell offers adults a sensitive and lively guide to deeper awareness of nature. Cornell's innovative nature awareness techniques combine with stunning photographs and quotations from famous naturalists to enliven your experience of nature. This new edition has been extensively rewritten and includes dozens of new photographs and quotations.

"A splendid masterpiece that captures the 'Oneness' we are all seeking to achieve with Nature."

—**Tom Brown, Jr.,** Founder of Living Tree Educational Foundation, author of *The Tracker*

AUM: The Melody of Love

AUM is God's tangible presence in creation. By hearing the Cosmic Sound, conscious contact with Spirit is established. Saint Francis described celestial AUM as "music so sweet and beautiful that, had it lasted a moment longer, I would have melted away from the sheer joy of it."

AUM is vibrating blissfully in every atom in the universe; when one listens to it, he enters into the stream of God's love. Communion with AUM expands one's consciousness and unites him with Spirit.

"Cornell invites us, through AUM, into the very source of nature, the fount of universal religious experience, and the essential experience of self. This intriguing book could very well change the way you see everything."

—**Garth Gilchrist,** nature writer, storyteller, portrayer of John Muir

Crystal Clarity Publishers offers a great number of additional resources to assist you on your life journey, including many other books, and a wide variety of inspirational and relaxation music and videos. To find out more information, please contact us at:

www.crystalclarity.com
14618 Tyler Foote Road / Nevada City, CA 95959
TOLL FREE 800.424.1055 or 530.478.7600
FAX: 530.478.7610
EMAIL: clarity@crystalclarity.com